~ In ~

Mother's Kitchen

In
Mother's
Kitchen

CELEBRATED WOMEN CHEFS
SHARE BELOVED FAMILY RECIPES

Featuring Lidia Bastianich, Gale Gand,

Sara Moulton, Alice Waters, *and Many More*

ANN COOPER *and* LISA HOLMES

RIZZOLI
NEW YORK

PREVIOUS SPREAD: Gale Gand with her grandmother and mother.
OPPOSITE: Katy Keck and family.
PAGE 8: Alison Awerbuch's mother's recipes.
PAGE 9: Anne Quatrano's Easy Bake Oven.
PAGE 12, FROM TOP: Coleen Donnelly, Cat Cora,
and Audrey Lennon (center) with her mother (left) and sisters.
PAGE 13: Amy Scherber (bottom right) and friends.
PAGE 239, FROM TOP: Katy Keck and mother,
Lisa M. Holmes with her mother and brother.

First published in the United States of America in 2005
by Rizzoli International Publications, Inc.
300 Park Avenue South, New York, NY 10010
www.rizzoliusa.com

© 2005 Ann Cooper and Lisa M. Holmes

2005 2006 2007 2008 / 10 9 8 7 6 5 4 3 2 1

Printed in the United States of America

DESIGNED BY PATRICIA FABRICANT

ISBN: 0-8478-2691-0

Library of Congress Catalog Control Number: 2005900956

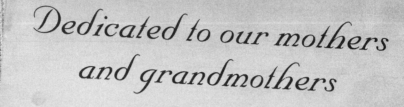

*Dedicated to our mothers
and grandmothers*

Contents

Introduction
∾ Ann Cooper and Lisa M. Holmes ∾

We originally conceived of this book while writing another book, *Bitter Harvest*, back in 2000. During our research for that project we learned just how few American children sit down to a family meal on a regular basis (a mere 15 percent). It was a figure that both frightened and disheartened us. As chefs we feared the loss of our nation's great culinary heritage, and as women with deep family and cultural ties we couldn't imagine a world in which the kitchen would no longer be the heart of the home. Food has always brought families together to create a sense of shared history. The flavors and aromas of a family's cultural kitchen create traditions and memories that are unique to that family. Recipes are treasured and passed down so that future generations will have a connection to their family's past. We set out to create a cookbook that would help to preserve some of these traditions.

A similar motivation spurred us to become professional chefs in the first place. We were driven by a longing to nourish others, to build on the foodways of our past, and to forge new food traditions. The vast majority of the women chefs we knew shared our feelings, and talking with them inspired us to build a cookbook honoring accomplished women chefs and the recipes passed down from, created for, or influenced by their mothers.

The time-consuming process of interviewing these chefs, our friends and colleagues, began and we quickly realized that there was much more to convey than just directions for how to make their heirloom recipes. Their stories were far more engaging and warm-hearted than we could ever have imagined. Many of the chefs enjoyed their trips down memory lane so much that they inundated us with recipes and the rituals associated with the

TO MY DARLING DAUGHTER
ALISON

With Love

1981

preparation and presentation of the dishes. There were secret tips and techniques that mothers confided in their children and emotions swelled in the telling of each story. We confirmed what we already knew— women cook from the heart, and our book honoring the chefs and the women who inspired them to become chefs wouldn't be whole without their stories.

Being a woman in a field still overwhelmingly dominated by men is a challenge. Many of the chefs in this book came to the profession later in life or after having started out on a completely different career path. We tell their stories as inspiration, not just for young women who are thinking of becoming chefs, but for women of any age who are contemplating a change to a career out of the expected.

The recipes included here are as magical and magnanimous as the women themselves and are based on flavor and a realness, or an earthiness, that cannot be found among the plates of show food found at so many restaurants. These recipes are about food that is meant to be shared among loved ones, without pretension or fussiness of presentation. The recipes reflect America's regional cuisines as well as the culinary diversity of each chef's unique heritage. *In Mother's Kitchen* is a medley of dishes inspired by traditional Northeastern, Southwestern, Midwestern, Southern, and Californian cuisines and enhanced by the flavors of Europe, Asia, and Africa. Whether the recipes have been created anew or learned at a grandmother's hand, all are united by their roots in a woman's urge to feed her family and friends.

Each of the chefs featured in this book has been nourished both physically and emotionally by food prepared by the maternal figures in her life—mothers, stepmothers, grandmothers, and aunts alike. Our intention, and sincere hope, is that you, too, will derive comfort, pleasure, and satiety from the stories and recipes presented on these pages. Through these women's recipes and stories we invite you to discover ways in which food from your family's history can be preserved and treasured for generations to come. Remember your mothers and grandmothers and allow yourself to be inspired to create new family recipes and traditions to be passed down to your daughters and granddaughters.

Matzo Cake
❧ Ann Cooper ❧

This is my family's favorite dessert and when we start eating it we instantly begin talking about my grandmother (pictured below), who would make it for every big occasion. My grandfather had his special part in the process too. I can still close my eyes and see him fastening an old-fashioned grinder to the family table, grinding the nuts and chocolate, and tasting the Manischewitz.

SERVES 8 TO 12

6 eggs, separated
1 cup sugar
Pinch salt
1 teaspoon vanilla
¼ cup kosher concord grape wine
½ cup matzo meal

½ cup grated dark chocolate
½ cup finely chopped almonds
1 rounded tablespoon unsweetened cocoa
1 teaspoon baking powder

1 Preheat the oven to 350° F and grease an 8-inch round layer cake pan.

2 On the highest speed of an electric mixer, beat the egg whites to stiff peaks. Slowly add the sugar.

3 In a separate bowl beat the egg yolks well. Add salt, vanilla, and wine and mix to combine.

4 Add the egg yolk mixture to the egg whites and mix well on medium speed.

5 One tablespoon at a time, add matzo meal, chocolate, almonds, and cocoa while mixing well on low speed. Mix in baking powder.

6 Pour the batter into the prepared cake pan and bake for 30 to 35 minutes, testing for doneness after 20 to 25 minutes. The cake is done when the top stops moving and the cake starts to pull away from the sides of the pan. When cool, the cake will pull farther away from the sides and the top will have a slight crust.

Caldo Verde
❧ Lisa M. Holmes ❧

My Portuguese great grandmother stood less than five feet tall and knew only a few choice words of English, but she held the family together in a way that was awe-inspiring. She was strong, but soft-hearted. She would chase my cousins and me around the house with a fly swatter yelling "Sonamabeech, you damn keeds!" We could see her grinning though, as she ran after us, keeping just one step behind. To this day, more than a decade after her death, she is still a presence in our family's home. One of her favorite dishes was this kale soup. She loved vegetables and would always have a pot of this on the stove when my family visited.

SERVES 12

2 tablespoons olive oil
1 medium Spanish onion, diced
2 cloves garlic, minced
2 pounds Idaho potatoes, peeled and coarsely chopped
1 pound carrots, peeled and coarsely chopped
3 to 4 parsnips (about 12 ounces), peeled and coarsely chopped
1 large smoked ham hock or smoked ham steak
1½ pounds kale, stemmed and chopped or julienned
3 quarts chicken stock
Salt and freshly ground black pepper to taste

1 In an 8-quart stock pot heat the olive oil and sauté the onion and garlic until tender.

2 Add the potatoes, carrots, and parsnips and stir.

3 Add the ham hock, kale (don't worry if it seems like a lot, it should fill the pot and will cook down when the soup simmers), and 2½ quarts of chicken stock. Reserve the remaining ½ quart for later use.

4 Cover the pot and simmer for at least an hour. When the root vegetables are cooked, roughly mash them using a slotted spoon and a fork. If your soup needs more liquid, add the remaining ½ quart of stock and return to a simmer. Season with salt and pepper to taste and serve.

Mom's Secret
This soup can also be made with beef stock and a beef bone. Either version freezes well.

Acknowledgments

IN ADDITION TO THE CHEFS who so generously gave us their recipes and shared their stories we would like to thank the mothers who gave their precious time and energy to taste and test recipes— Pam Abbs, Heather Hecox, Stephanie Jackson, Alice Legarde, Liz Shulkin Jodi Walker, and Shelly Wiesner. We also extend our heartfelt thanks to our gracious and enthusiastic editor, Christopher Steighner, who made this project especially enjoyable and to our talented and tireless agent, Lisa Ekus, without whom this book may never have seen the light of day. Kudos to the book's designer, Patricia Fabricant, for tying everything together in such a lovely package.

As well we would like to thank our families—especially little Ben, who not only had to give up time with his mother while she worked, but who also had to make accommodations for a new baby sister during the writing of this book. His warmth and gentle spirit are his mother's greatest inspiration.

~ *In* ~
Mother's
Kitchen

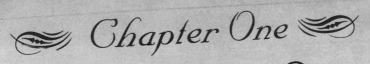

Chapter One
Mothers & Grandmothers

HISTORICALLY AND TRADITIONALLY, women have embodied the spirit of the kitchen, particularly in the home. Virtually every cook or chef attributes a love of food to his or her mother or grandmother. Their passion for food is based on the traditions of family, giving, and nurturing. We have heard scores of stories about women cooking with their mothers and grandmothers or mimicking them as they cooked in their own "Easy Bake Ovens." Over and over they expressed their beliefs that food, love, and life are inextricably entwined. As they grew up, they were nurtured with good, wholesome food. In turn, these women have built lives and careers in professional kitchens in an effort to pass on the feelings and lessons learned in the kitchens of their youth.

This chapter brings together a diverse group of women who were all strongly influenced by their mothers' or grandmothers' cooking. Longteine de Monteiro shares two of her mother's Cambodian recipes, and Ann Cashion fondly remembers a dish that she and her mother bonded over, Dried Lima Beans. Ana Sortun lovingly recreates her mom's Crab Melt, which she remembers eating with tomato soup as a child, and Lidia Bastianich recalls a dish straight out of her grandmother's colorful Italian repertoire. There are, of course, many more, all from a wide range of cultural traditions, and they all represent the love of a mother or grandmother to a daughter or granddaughter.

Giant Prawns with Daikon
Longteine de Monteiro
ELEPHANT WALK, BOSTON AND CAMBRIDGE
CARAMBOLA, WALTHAM, MASSACHUSETTS

Longteine de Monteiro (pictured with her mother, Nadsa, below and opposite), chef/owner of The Elephant Walk and Carambola restaurants in Boston and Cambridge, Massachusetts, grew up in Cambodia surrounded by flavorful food prepared by her mother's cooks. She didn't learn to cook as a child but was always tasting everything—including the servants' food. She was obsessed with the flavors of her native country. She married, at 18 had two children, and spent a couple of more years in Cambodia before she began living abroad with her husband, who worked in foreign affairs at that time. After stints in Yugoslavia, the Philippines, and Taiwan, and a final move to France, the fall of Cambodia's government left her husband out of work. Longteine, who had been supervising the cooking in her family's kitchens over the years, had learned quite a bit about Cambodian cooking and resolved that the only way to survive was to open a restaurant in the south of France. For ten years Longteine was the only cook in her fifty-five-seat restaurant, while her husband worked the front of the house. In 1990 the couple moved to the United States and opened the first Elephant Walk, serving French-Cambodian food,

in 1991. The original restaurant outgrew its space, and currently Longteine and her family run three independent establishments. The following recipes are ones that Longteine fondly remembers learning to cook as a teenager with her mother.

2 TO 4 SERVINGS

1 tablespoon mushroom soy sauce
1½ teaspoons fish sauce
½ teaspoon salt
½ teaspoon freshly ground black
    pepper
8 giant prawns, peeled and
    deveined
1 cup preserved daikon radish,
    rinsed *(see note)*
3 tablespoons vegetable oil
3 garlic cloves, smashed and
    coarsely chopped
3 tablespoons sugar
2½ cups chicken broth

1 In a medium bowl, mix together the soy sauce, fish sauce, salt, and ground black pepper. Add the prawns, turn them over, and set aside to marinate for 10 minutes. Meanwhile, thinly slice the daikon radish on a diagonal and soak it in several cups of water to remove the saltiness, if necessary. Drain.

2 Heat the oil in a large heavy skillet over medium high-heat and sauté the garlic until golden, about 5 to 10 seconds. Reduce the heat to medium, add the sugar, and cook, stirring constantly, for about 2 minutes, as it liquefies, turns brown, and becomes frothy.

3 Add the prawns and stir to coat with the garlic and caramelized sugar. Add the chicken broth and bring to a boil. Add the daikon slices, return to a boil, stirring occasionally, and continue cooking for about 5 minutes, until the prawns are opaque. Remove from the heat and serve immediately.

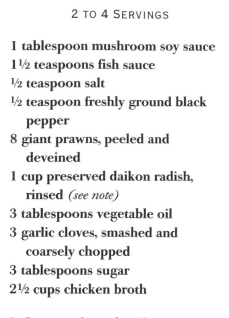

Mom's Secret You can find all of the unusual ingredients in this and the following recipe—including smoke fish powder, kaffir lime leaves, galangal, and preserved daikon—at Asian specialty markets. Fresh ginger may be substituted for galangal.

Pork with Pineapple

Longteine de Monteiro

ELEPHANT WALK, BOSTON AND CAMBRIDGE
CARAMBOLA, WALTHAM, MASSACHUSETTS

SERVES 4 TO 6

PASTE
3 dried New Mexico chilies, soaked,
    seeded, and deveined
1 stalk lemongrass, thinly sliced
4 cloves garlic, coarsely chopped
2 large shallots, coarsely chopped
10 kaffir lime leaves, deveined *(see note,
    page 19)*
2 tablespoons chopped fresh cilantro
    stems
1 tablespoon peeled and coarsely
    chopped galangal *(see note)*
¼ teaspoon turmeric

¼ cup vegetable oil
2½ cups unsweetened coconut milk
2 pounds spareribs or baby back ribs, cut
    into 1½-inch lengths and split, or 1½-
    pounds fresh ham, cut into 2-inch pieces
2 teaspoons shrimp paste
¼ cup sugar
2 tablespoons fish sauce
2 teaspoons salt
1 small underripe pineapple (about 1
    pound), peeled, cored, and julienned
¼ cup Asian smoke fish powder *(see note)*
6 kaffir lime leaves, deveined *(see note)*
2 tablespoons fresh lime juice
Fresh basil leaves, for garnish

1   Make a paste by blending the chilies, lemongrass, garlic, shallots, kaffir leaves, cilantro stems, galangal, turmeric, and 1 cup of water in a blender or food processor and processing until smooth—approximately 2 to 3 minutes. Set aside.

2   Heat the oil in a large skillet over medium-high heat. Add 1 cup of coconut milk and the reserved paste and cook, stirring constantly, until the aroma of the spices is fully developed, about 5 minutes.

3   Stir in the pork, shrimp paste, sugar, fish sauce, and salt and cook again for 5 minutes. Add 2 cups of water and the remaining 1½ cups of coconut milk and bring to a boil. Reduce the heat to low, add the pineapple, and simmer for 10 more minutes. Add the Asian smoke fish powder and kaffir lime leaves and cook until the pork is tender, about 5 to 10 minutes more. Remove from the heat.

4   Stir in the lime juice, garnish with basil leaves, and serve with rice.

Roast Chicken Hash with Poached Eggs and Herbed Hollandaise

Kerry L. Heffernan

THE FAIRMONT HOTEL, SAN FRANCISCO

Kerry Heffernan found her way to a professional kitchen out of necessity—she was broke! Her uncles owned restaurants, including a couple of pizzerias, where she would sit on a stool picking at the mozzarella and raw pizza dough while she listened to their stories. At eighteen when she moved from Los Angeles to San Francisco with only $500 and a couple of pairs of jeans to her name, she was able to spin a well-educated lie about her experience to get her first job in a pizzeria. Back in Los Angeles, she worked alongside a Latino cook who yelled "mira! mira!" at her so much that she thought it was her nickname. It wasn't until later that she found out that mira means "look" in Spanish! Eager to work at the Beverly Hills Hotel, Kerry kept showing up, hoping they would hire her. First they said she didn't have any uniforms, so she got her mother to buy her some chef's jackets. Another time they said she didn't have any tools, so she begged and borrowed enough to buy some knives. The chef kept putting her off, telling her she was "an idiot," until one day someone didn't show up for work and she got her foot in the door. Her position was far from lofty—she was the self-described "toast girl" on the breakfast shift and she loved it. Several restaurants later, including her own renowned Autumn Moon Café, she is now the executive sous-chef at the Fairmont Hotel in San Francisco.

This Roast Chicken Hash was one of Kerry's mom's specialties, and Kerry has served it in every restaurant where she has held a chef's position. Today it is on the menu at the Fairmont's Laurel Court Restaurant.

6 medium red-skinned potatoes

¼ cup corn oil

1 medium onion, julienned

¼ cup julienned pasilla peppers

½ cup julienned red bell peppers

2 tablespoons minced garlic

3 cups roasted chicken, cut into 1-inch pieces

1 teaspoon minced mixed fresh herbs, (thyme, oregano, and rosemary)

Salt and pepper to taste

12 poached eggs

1½ cups Herbed Hollandaise (recipe follows)

1 Preheat the oven to 400° F. In a large saucepan, cover the potatoes with lightly salted water. Bring to a boil and cook for about 10 minutes, just until tender. Drain and reserve the potatoes.

2 Heat the oil in a large cast-iron skillet. Add the onion and peppers and sauté over medium heat for 7 minutes. Add the garlic and sauté 1 more minute. Stir in the potatoes, chicken, and herbs. Salt and pepper the mixture to taste, then mash it slightly with a fork or potato masher. Allow the mixture to become golden and get slightly crispy; turn over and brown on the other side.

3 Serve at once with poached eggs and Herbed Hollandaise.

HERBED HOLLANDAISE

SERVES 12

9 egg yolks

2 tablespoons warm water

¾ pound (3 sticks) unsalted butter, melted

Dash Tabasco (to taste)

2 tablespoons fresh lemon juice

6 tablespoons minced mixed fresh herbs (tarragon, chives, Italian parsley, and basil work well)

Kosher salt to taste

1 Place the egg yolks and warm water in a medium-size stainless steel bowl.

2 Over a double boiler, whisk the egg yolks continuously until they start to thicken and you can see the bottom of the bowl in between strokes, like a thickening whipped cream (7 to 10 minutes). Do not stop whisking! If yolks start to cook or look like scrambled eggs, remove the bowl while whisking and use the double boiler in short increments.

3 Slowly drizzle in the melted butter in a steady stream while continuing to whisk. Add the Tabasco, lemon juice, herbs, and salt. Serve 2-ounce side portions per person with Roast Chicken Hash (see recipe above).

⊰ KITCHEN MEMORIES ⊱

I can't smell the aroma of fresh sage without thinking about riding horses up in the ranch-land. That smell, to me, is like living that style of life. The smell of fresh parsley is the smell of my grandmother's hands—she'd always be chopping up parsley to put in something. I have so many food memories like that. A Valencia orange—whenever I smell one that isn't broken open yet, it reminds me of being poked by thorns while climbing trees. Have you ever seen avocado leaves? A big, full avocado grove of 500 avocado trees in the summertime is so dense, you can't see through it, and the trees are really strong and easy to climb. I do think that my experience of growing up in a rural environment set the stage for me.

Mom's cooking style was healthful. Nothing was ever fried or greasy. She grew up on a farm in upstate New York in Spring Valley, where they had fresh eggs in the morning and all that stuff. She was a really great cook. Her manicotti was fabulous. She made flank steak that I loved. She used different cuts of meat that weren't typical, and she always used to try to get us to eat liver by putting Marsala sauce on it or something. My brother was allergic to chocolate and her way of dealing with that was to tell me that I was allergic to chocolate as well, so I think the first time I ate chocolate was when I was twelve. Our snacks were always fresh fruit, dried fruit, nuts, pieces of cheese. We didn't ever have Ding Dongs or Yoo Hoos. I can remember back when I was seven, having horse-radish cream on my roast beef and thinking that was fabulous. My brother and I would always want to go to the Crackerboard and get Jarlsberg cheese when everyone else wanted to get hamburgers. My friends all thought we were nuts.

Mom's Secret It is very important to get the hash a bit crispy, and that's why we use a good heavy cast-iron pan, to get an even low heat that doesn't sear but gently browns the hash.

Dorothy Jane's Sautéed White Fish
with Tartar Sauce
❧ *Cindy Pawlcyn* ❧

CINDY'S BACKSTREET KITCHEN, ST. HELENA, CALIFORNIA
MUSTARDS GRILL, YOUNTVILLE, CALIFORNIA

Cindy Pawlcyn first started cooking because it made her dad happy. He preferred gifts that were made, not purchased, and since Cindy had older siblings with talents in music and art, she headed for the kitchen, where she felt most at home. The fact that her father loved eating and was willing to try anything made it fun for Cindy, and by the time she turned thirteen, she was enrolled in formal cooking classes at a local kitchen shop in her home state of Minnesota. When chefs like Paula Wolfert, Julia Child, and Jacques Pepin published new books they often visited the school on book tours as special guest teachers, and Cindy served as an assistant. Cindy graduated from high school and earned her degree in cooking from the trade school at roughly the same time, then went to college for a degree in hotel and restaurant management.

At age twenty she landed a job at Chicago's Le Perroquet and then opened a slew of restaurants, including Mustards, which has now been in operation for twenty-two years. Her current venture, Cindy's Backstreet Kitchen, is located in the Napa Valley and features American cuisine, some of which harkens back to old favorites from her mom (pictured above with Cindy's grandmother).

Mom's Secret You can use any of a variety of freshwater firm-fleshed fish in this recipe. Northern, walleye, and sunfish may be unfamiliar to those who grew up far from the Midwest; these fish thrive in the cold lakes of states like Minnesota.

1 cup all-purpose flour (approximately)
1 teaspoon salt
½ teaspoon freshly ground black pepper
18 sunfish, dressed, or 6 ounces each of very fresh pike, northern,

or walleye fillets (*see note*)
⅛ to ¼ cup vegetable or canola oil

Mom's Tartar Sauce (recipe follows)
Lemon wedges

1 Season the flour with salt and pepper and place the flour mixture in a brown paper bag. Add the fish and shake.

2 Heat the oil in a cast-iron pan. Remove the fish from the bag, shaking off excess flour as you go, and cook until golden brown and crisp on the outside, moist and tender on the inside. Serve with Mom's Tartar Sauce and lemon wedges.

MOM'S TARTAR SAUCE

MAKES 2 CUPS

1½ cups Hellmann's Real Mayonnaise
1 shake Worcestershire sauce
2 to 3 shakes Tabasco
Juice of ½ lemon
1 to 2 tablespoons capers, rinsed and chopped

2 tablespoons minced sweet pickles or finely chopped cornichons
1 tablespoon minced chives or tarragon
1 teaspoon Dijon mustard
1 scallion, minced

Combine all of the ingredients and mix well. Serve immediately or refrigerate.

⊰ KITCHEN MEMORIES ⊱

My mom's fish were cooked with the skin on—so delicious! We had a variety of freshwater fish, depending on what my dad caught—pike, walleye, "sunnies," big-mouth bass, or perch. My job would be to clean the fish with Dad and cook them with Mom. We liked the "sunnies" best cooked on the bone, because the meat was the sweetest, plus we could eat them with our fingers! My dad was an avid hunter and raised chickens and ducks in the backyard—and we lived in suburbia! So we were exposed to everything; we had things like blood sausage on a regular basis. My dad was Russian and Austrian, and my mom was Norwegian and German, and they cooked, and you ate what was served, and you learned to like it.

Chicken and Dumplings
Lisa Schroeder
MOTHER'S BISTRO & BAR, PORTLAND, OREGON

Lisa Schroeder is the chef/owner of Mother's Bistro & Bar in Portland, Oregon. Lisa's mother, Belle, was a wonderful cook. She had a restaurant before Lisa was born and was a successful businesswoman and restaurateur at a time when few women worked at all. Though Lisa never got to see her in action at her restaurant, she has heard some wonderful stories that inspire her in her own business. Belle never actually taught Lisa how to cook, but she did teach her how to appreciate good food, and although Belle never got to see Lisa's restaurant, her picture hangs in the restaurant, watching over the kitchen. "If nothing else," Lisa says, "the vibrant taste memories that she bestowed upon me live on in my food."

The following dish is one of the most popular at Mother's Bistro & Bar. Lisa believes it's "probably because nearly everyone remembers their own mother's or grandmother's version of this dish. Some mothers made 'slippery' dumplings, but ours are more biscuit-like. Unfortunately, many mothers out there used a biscuit mix, so very few people can remember dumplings as tender and delicious as these." This recipe calls for Belle's Chicken Noodle Soup (page 188), and the chicken used to make the broth in that recipe, so it's like getting two different meals for the price of one!

SERVES 8

1½ gallons (6 quarts) Belle's Chicken
  Noodle Soup (page 188),
  without the noodles or matzoh balls,
  meat reserved
1 cup (2 sticks) unsalted butter
2 cups all-purpose flour

DUMPLINGS
3 cups all-purpose flour
1 tablespoon baking powder
½ tablespoon salt
4 tablespoons finely chopped fresh
  Italian parsley
2 tablespoons cold unsalted butter,
  cut into ½-inch pieces
1¼ cups whole milk
Salt and freshly ground black pepper
  to taste

1 In a large pot, bring the chicken soup to a boil.

2 While the soup is heating, make the roux. In a heavy-bottomed saucepan or sauté pan, melt the butter over medium heat. Add the flour and mix with a whisk to ensure that there are no lumps. Cook over medium heat while stirring with a wooden spoon for about 5 minutes, until the mixture resembles sand on the beach. It should be light beige in color and not at all browned.

3 Add the roux to the hot soup while whisking to ensure that there are no lumps. Return the mixture to a boil, lower the heat, and continue simmering for 15 to 20 minutes, stirring frequently with a wooden spoon to ensure there are no lumps and the bottom does not scorch. As the soup simmers, be sure to skim any scum that rises to the top.

4 While the broth and roux mixture simmer, make the dumpling dough: Combine the flour, baking powder, salt, and 2 tablespoons of the parsley in a bowl, and using a pastry blender, whisk, or fork, cut in the butter until the mixture resembles coarse meal. It's okay if there are a few visible pieces of butter—that will yield a flaky, tender biscuit. Add the milk and stir briefly to blend. Do not overmix or the dumplings will be chewy.

5 Dip a small ice cream scoop into the dumpling mixture and drop the scooped dough into the simmering soup. Repeat until all the dumpling batter has been used. Cover the pot and simmer until the dumplings are done, about 20 minutes. Try not to lift the lid as the dumplings are cooking, or you will slow down the cooking process.

6 Put the cooked chicken in the pot with the hot dumpling mixture. Stir gently, season with salt and pepper, return to a simmer, and cook for 5 more minutes. Using a long-handled serving spoon or tongs, lift out the chicken pieces and dumplings and place them in serving bowls. Ladle some chicken gravy on top of the dumplings and chicken, sprinkle with the remaining fresh chopped Italian parsley, and serve.

Mom's Crab Melt
Ana Sortun
OLEANA, BOSTON

Ana Sortun, (pictured with her mother, left) now chef/owner of Oleana in Boston, caught the cooking bug at about fourteen years old, when she landed her first restaurant job. The owners of that restaurant must have seen a spark in Ana because they sent her to take some cooking class. It wasn't long before she began working at the cooking school and came to the early conclusion that cooking was her destiny. As a young teenager she decided to attend cooking school and forego college. To prepare she took private French lessons three times a week for two and a half years until she was able to pass the fluency exam necessary to gain entrance to La Varenne École de Cuisine in Paris, where she earned a degree in culinary arts. Her studies in wine at L'Academie du Vin earned her a second degree. Upon her return to the United States, her first stop was Seattle. The restaurant scene was slow there at that time, so after a year she headed east, to Boston, where she picked up a catering job and some work as a private chef on a yacht. Not long afterward she embarked on a journey through the Mediterranean, where she spent time in a variety of kitchens before returning to Massachusetts to begin working toward her ultimate goal of owning a restaurant. Oleana is now four years old.

This recipe is a variation on a crab melt her mother used to make. Ana grew up in Seattle and remembers making this with Dungeness crab and eating it with a bowl of tomato soup.

2 cups heavy cream

2 tablespoons brandy or ¼ cup white wine

Pinch fennel seed

1 bunch scallions

1 pound Maine crabmeat

2 cups grated Asiago cheese

Salt and pepper to taste

4 English muffins, toasted

1 Preheat the oven to broil.

2 In a large saucepan over medium heat, combine the cream, brandy, and fennel seed and simmer until reduced by half.

3 Clean the scallions and cut them into 1-inch pieces. Stir into the cream mixture.

4 Squeeze any excess water out of the crab and fold into the cream mixture. Stir in the cheese. Season with salt and pepper to taste.

5 Smear the mixture onto toasted English muffins and broil for a minute or two, until bubbly.

⊰ KITCHEN MEMORIES ⊱

My mom was a simple cook, but she was a great cook. She grew up on a farm so she was ingredient driven. She really knew what fresh was and what good was, so we ate well. We ate good, fresh home-made food, not canned or frozen. My grandmother was also an excellent cook and made everything: cinnamon rolls, everything. Nothing was bought. If she made stuffing or mashed potatoes, she used homemade bread and real potatoes. Both my mother and my grandmother taught me that it's really about ingredients and less about what you do with them that makes food taste good. One of my favorite things my mom made was crab melts. She would also make really good fried chicken and great beef stroganoff! She was a great baker and made really good German chocolate cake, brownies, and caramel apples. My grandmother always had fresh rolls, home-made ice cream, and homemade butter.

Stracciatella alla Romana

ROMAN "EGG DROP" SOUP

Lidia Bastianich

FELIDIA & BECCO, NEW YORK
LIDIA'S ITALY, PITTSBURGH & KANSAS CITY, MISSOURI

From the moment she was born, Lidia Bastianich led a life inspired by things culinary. She remembers her maternal grandmother's kitchen in Italy always being open to the local field workers, and a perpetual pot of something simmering there for them. As a child, Lidia watched them eating in the courtyard around big wooden tables and remembers her grandparents' property as rich with culinary delights. There were olive trees, wheat fields, potato fields, and grapevines. They made their own olive oil, sent wheat to be ground into flour, harvested potatoes that would last all winter, dried their own beans, and made raisins from all the best grapes. Of course they also made wine, and every November her family slaughtered a pig, rendered bacon, and made prosciutto.

Lidia's aunt was a private chef for a local family and Lidia helped her aunt plan some of their meals. She remembers "going to the markets and choosing the smallest salad greens, seeing the pheasants and rabbits that were hanging, and then coming home and helping her to pluck them, to burn the hairs away. I got into the meals and the beauty of working with food on a whole new level."

In 1958, Lidia's family immigrated to the United States. Her mother was an elementary school teacher, her father a mechanic, and initially Lidia thought she might pursue a career in medicine. Throughout her education, however, she was drawn to restaurant work to earn pocket money, and along the way she met and married her husband who was, naturally, in the restaurant business. In 1971 he expressed a desire to open his own restaurant, and Lidia volunteered to help out. They hired an Italian-American chef and Lidia went to work alongside him. She knew the food her Italian-American chef was serving was good, but it wasn't real Italian cuisine, and at the end of ten years, they sold their restaurants and opened Felidia, with Lidia at the helm.

In spite of her own love for the business, Lidia encouraged her children away from the culinary world. Little did she know they'd both return to work at her side. And Lidia's mother still has an apartment at Lidia's house, where she now helps her grandchildren and great grandchildren. Lidia says, "So, you know, four generations— we've done it together." The following recipe has been a favorite of many generations.

SERVES 6

6 cups strained and defatted chicken stock
Salt to taste
Freshly ground black pepper to taste
3 cups fresh spinach, stemmed, washed,
   and cut into ½-inch strips

3 eggs
⅓ cup freshly grated Parmigiano-
   Reggiano cheese, plus more for
   sprinkling over the soup

1 Bring the chicken stock to a boil and season lightly with salt and pepper. Stir in the spinach and cook until wilted, about 1 minute.

2 Meanwhile, beat the eggs with a good grinding of black pepper until thoroughly blended. Beat in the grated cheese. Pour the egg mixture into the simmering soup while stirring constantly to break it into "little rags." Continue to cook, stirring for 1 minute, until egg is fully cooked. Check the seasoning, sprinkle with additional Parmesan cheese, and serve immediately.

KITCHEN MEMORIES

Straciatella mean "little rags" in Italian, which is what the strands of beaten eggs cooked in the broth resemble. Eggs, so fresh they were still warm from the chicken or duck, were a cherished food as well as a good source of nourishment when I was growing up. We enjoyed them all ways, even raw. (My grandfather, Giovanni, would eat them still warm by puncturing a little hole in the egg and sipping the egg right from the shell.) One of my favorites was a whipped zabaglione with black coffee—it was a breakfast treat. Our merende—morning snack—was often a frittata of some type or eggs whisked into a simple soup, like this one. Eggs were used in making pasta dough or dropped in the pasta as a condiment.

When I make brodo—a clear soup with a little something in it—I think of my father. He loved all kinds of soup, but especially these simple and elegant ones. My father was a very proper man who insisted on beautiful place settings and crisp linens. When we were young, my grandmother made this soup with duck eggs, chicken eggs, or even goose eggs—whichever type was freshest. Prepared without the spinach, this is a perfect soup for children.

My Mother's Dried Lima Beans
≈ *Ann Cashion* ≈

CASHION'S EAT PLACE & JOHNNY'S HALF SHELL, WASHINGTON, D.C.

Ann Cashion (pictured with her mother, left) grew up in Jackson, Mississippi, in the 1950s and 1960s. There wasn't even a pizzeria in her town until she was a teenager, so home food was a huge part of her Southern culture. Though she didn't cook much with her mother until she was a junior in high school, Ann was a self-described "eater," who bonded with her mother in her love for various foods that the other members of her family didn't particularly like. Ann was flying through her PhD program in English literature and living in San Francisco with hopes of teaching when she started cooking a lot at home. She dropped out of school and took a job at a bakery in the East Bay area; she was making no money but had found her passion and never looked back.

After a year at the bakery, Ann headed off to Florence, where she learned to roll pasta with a 4 foot long rolling pin and was schooled in the finer points of wood-fired cookery. She eventually moved to Washington, D.C., where she worked with Nora Poullion and worked up the courage to open her first restaurant. Today Ann is the owner of Cashion's Eat Place, now ten years old, and Johnny's Half Shell, in its sixth year. The food at Johnny's is theme oriented, but at Cashion's Eat Place it's "aggressively seasonal," with a focus on "traditional preparations" like this recipe for her mother's peasant-style lima beans.

Mom's Secret My mother generally uses the meat remaining on the bone of a whole ham. I rarely have that luxury. I have often substituted ham hocks or even slab bacon. If substituting bacon, render four or five slices until golden brown, but not crisp, in the olive oil prior to sautéing the onions.

SERVES 8 TO 10

1 pound dried lima beans, preferably
  Camellia brand *(see note)*
3 tablespoons olive oil
1 medium onion, diced
½ pound ham, from a whole ham,
  cut into large cubes

1 head garlic, cut in half crosswise
2 bay leaves
Salt and pepper to taste

1 Rinse and sort the beans. Do not soak.

2 Heat the oil in a heavy-bottomed saucepan. Sauté the onion until translucent. Add the beans, ham, garlic, bay leaves, and water to cover.

3 Season with salt and pepper. Bring to a simmer and cook gently, for about 1½ hours, until beans are tender and beginning to break down. You will probably need to add water several times during this process.

4 Remove the garlic and bay leaves before serving.

Mom's Secret My mother has convinced me that Camellia brand are the ideal beans for this recipe, and I generally pick some up when I'm in Mississippi. You can find them on the web at www.camelliabrand.com

⊰ KITCHEN MEMORIES ⊱

One bond I had with my mother, although we didn't prepare food much together, was a similar love for some types of foods that no one else in my family liked, and she would make these things knowing that I was the only one who was going to enjoy them. For instance, my mother had a serious iron deficiency, so she often used to make these enormous white lima beans with ham in them, a very, very plain, sort of peasant-like food. I was the only other person in the family who ate them because I just loved them, so it was our little thing. It was the same with liver, for the same reason—she had to eat a lot of it. Of course my brothers and sisters totally rejected the liver. I loved some of the more difficult vegetables like okra, so she'd always make a little pot and not serve them to anyone else in the family because they made my younger sister sick.

My Mother's Cabbage and Noodles
❧ Rozanne Gold ❧

When Rozanne was four she carried a little cookbook everywhere she went (even to the bathroom!), and as she grew, she continued to read cookbooks and explore the world of food and travel. She loved experimenting with food and once, early in the morning while her parents were sleeping, she even tried to re-create a scene out of Heidi by melting a chunk of Swiss cheese over an open flame in her family's kitchen. The smell of roasting stinky cheese at 6 A.M. brought a pair of bewildered, sleepy-eyed parents running. Later she impressed her friends with duck à l'orange and popovers. As a family Rozanne and her parents loved dining out so much that they often found new restaurants before the critics did. One of their favorite special-occasion spots was New York City's Rainbow Room. Her father nearly burst with pride when Rozanne became the restaurant's consulting chef in 1987, a post she held until the end of 1999.

Never professionally trained, Rozanne has an unwavering entrepreneurial spirit. It first shone through when she was eleven years old and started a children's day camp with a friend. At age sixteen, she took her first restaurant job and started bartending (illegally) at Old London Fishery in Queens, and though she went to college and pursued a graduate degree in human sexuality at Tufts University, she dropped out, deciding that food and cooking were much more exciting. As a self-described "foodie," in 1975 Gold's life was a swirl of food-related activity. Her first paying restaurant kitchen job was at Café Tartufo in Manhattan. She soon became the first woman to work at the Colombe D'Or and picked up work at several other restaurants—all at the same time—before she landed a job working as Mayor Ed Koch's chef in 1978. During that time she cooked for countless presidents and prime ministers from around the globe.

The job with Mayor Koch was Rozanne's springboard, and today, Gold is an author (many of her books feature three-ingredient recipes), consultant, and television star.

Mom's Secret The secret is to squeeze the water from the shredded cabbage after it's salted and left to wilt, then cooking it in sweet butter until it becomes soft and dark golden in color. It's then tossed with egg noodles.

1 very large head green cabbage
Kosher salt
8 tablespoons (1 stick) unsalted butter

12 ounces medium-wide egg noodles
Freshly ground black pepper to taste

1 Cut the cabbage in half and remove the core. With a sharp knife, shred the cabbage into ¼-inch-wide slices. Place in a large colander and sprinkle heavily with kosher salt, using your hands to toss. Put a heavy object on top (a water-filled teakettle is perfect) to weight the cabbage down. Put the colander in a pan to collect any liquid or set it in the sink. Let it sit for 3 to 4 hours. Press down hard on the cabbage and squeeze with your fists to extract as much water as possible.

2 In a very large nonstick skillet, melt the butter and add the cabbage. Cook over medium heat, stirring frequently, for 30 to 40 minutes, until the cabbage is deep golden brown; it will shrink considerably. Lower the heat, if necessary, so that the cabbage does not burn.

3 Cook the noodles in a large pot of salted boiling water, until just tender, about 15 minutes. Drain the noodles thoroughly and place in a warm bowl. Add the hot cabbage and toss together so that the noodles are completely integrated with the cabbage. Add salt, if needed, and lots of freshly ground black pepper.

⇥ KITCHEN MEMORIES ⇤

My mother was a great cook. Her background was Hungarian on both sides. I didn't know this when I was growing up, but my maternal grandfather and grandmother, whose wedding ring I wear, had a small Hungarian restaurant in Astoria, Queens. It was on the second floor of a small storefront, where I guess she cooked and he waited tables when my mother was very very tiny. My mother doesn't remember much about it, but her food was always very lusty—great stuffed cabbage, and she's famous for her pot roast—and my comfort food is a cabbage-and-noodles dish she still makes for me when I go to her house today. It turns out that it was the original three-ingredient recipe.

 When I visit her in Queens, not far from where I grew up, I bring her one of my Venetian Wine Cakes. She buys me ice cream. My treat is that I can sit and eat all the pints of ice cream before I go home because I won't keep ice cream in my house. They're edible expressions of love from childhood that continue to this day.

Potatoes Boulangère
❧ *Anne Quatrano* ❧

BACCHANALIA, THE FLOATAWAY CAFÉ, AND STAR PROVISIONS, ATLANTA

Anne Quatrano (pictured opposite) describes the everyday food of her childhood as "tragic," due in no small part to the sudden and dramatic appearance of canned and frozen foods in the American marketplace. Her mother wasn't much of a cook, but both of her grandmothers were outstanding examples in the kitchen, and that's where Anne got her earliest inspirations. She decided early on that she wanted to own her own restaurant and realized that to be an effective owner, she should know the goings on of the back of the house. She enrolled in the California Culinary Academy and after graduation worked the front and back of the house for two years, before realizing that cooking came naturally to her. It was then that she made the final transition to working full time in the kitchen and moved to New York City.

It was a trial by fire, as she quickly found herself unexpectedly in the chef's position. She had a hard time finding reliable help and eventually hired her husband, Clifford, to work alongside her. They did well, earning two stars from the *New York Times* critic Craig Claiborne. From there Anne and Clifford moved through a number of New York City restaurants—it was the late 1980s, money was flowing freely, and the restaurant business in New York was booming. Anne and Clifford agreed to run the restaurant Grolier 8, opened and operated by a group of young, wealthy twenty-somethings who were good friends of theirs. It was located in the old Grolier Publishing house, which had been completely transformed—a restaurant on the first floor, and a different night club of increasing decadence on every ascending floor. For about a year and a half it was the place to see and be seen, but the owners, in spite of all the money they had, were inexperienced in the restaurant business, and the building was sold to a catering company. Anne and Clifford made a disappointing foray into the Hamptons before deciding to make the move to Atlanta, where they are the successful owners of Bacchanalia, The Floataway Café, and Star Provisions. Anne and Clifford grow as much of their own produce as they can and hope to reach a point where all the produce comes from their farm.

Anne's maternal grandmother made these potatoes with bits of country ham. Anne calls them Potatoes Boulangère, but her no-nonsense grandmother called them Potatoes with Ham.

SERVES 6

2 tablespoons olive oil
    (pure and unfiltered)
8 cloves garlic, thinly sliced
3 white onions, peeled and sliced
6 sprigs fresh thyme
Salt and pepper to taste
10 medium Yukon gold potatoes,
    peeled and very thinly sliced
2 cups hot chicken stock

1 Preheat the oven to 350° F. In a heavy-bottomed sauté pan, heat the oil and lightly sauté the garlic and onions until golden brown. Add the thyme and season with salt and pepper.

2 In a large baking dish, layer the potatoes and cooked onions, adding stock between layers and seasoning with salt and pepper.

3 Bake for about 2 hours, or until the potatoes are tender and golden brown.

⊰ KITCHEN MEMORIES ⊱

I used to come visit my mother's side of the family down here, and certainly there were some things from the South that were different to us. They made these potatoes here with ham, very brothy. My mother wasn't an incredible cook, but she was a health nut way before her time. She would drink half a cup of wheat germ with her orange juice every morning, and all the water she cooked her vegetables in she would strain and put in the fridge, and that would be her drinking water for the rest of the day. Very intelligent and a little wacky!

Margaret Waters' Granola
Alice Waters
CHEZ PANISSE AND CAFÉ FANNY, BERKELEY, CALIFORNIA

The name of Alice Waters (pictured, with her daughter, left), chef/owner of the now 34-year-old Chez Panisse, is practically synonymous with California. It's a long way from her Chatham, New Jersey, roots, as was France the first time she visited there at the age of nineteen. She fell in love with the food and says, "It was the first time I had really ever really eaten! Anything exotic at all, anything that was really about flavor, and it was . . . cooked in a way that suggested that there was some other purpose to eating other than just sort of fueling up."

When she got back, she wanted to eat the way she'd eaten in France every day, where she had visited farmer's markets and made friends with the local baker. She opened Chez Panisse in 1971 with a five-course, fixed-price menu that changed daily. Over three decades she has created a network of farmers who supply both the original restaurant, the upstairs café (opened in 1980), and Café Fanny (opened in 1983), located a few miles down the road, with high quality, organic produce. Alice is highly respected and admired by her peers; to culinary students around the world, Chez Panisse is a sort of Mecca to which they happily make pilgrimages every year.

Known for her Edible Schoolyard work in the Berkeley public schools, Alice continues to work hard to change the face of public school lunches through curriculum development and active on-site organic gardening. She continues to be heavily involved in the Horticulture Project at the San Francisco County Jail and its related program, the Garden Project, a market garden as well as a job-training program for inmates.

Alice shared this recipe from her mother who was always interested in good health. Although she didn't feel she had the time to be creative when cooking, Margaret Waters firmly believed in a good breakfast and whole grains. She thought this granola was a perfect breakfast for her children, because it was a little sweet, but still healthy.

1 cup honey

1 cup canola oil

1 pound rolled oats

1 cup sliced almonds

1 cup sunflower seeds

1 cup wheat germ

1 cup whole wheat flour

1 cup dry milk

1 Preheat the oven to 375° F.

2 Warm the honey and oil over low heat until liquefied. Combine the dry ingredients and stir in the honey and oil until fully incorporated.

3 Spread the mixture in a thin layer on two 12 x 18" sheet pans, and bake for 20 minutes. Remove from the oven and toss immediately. Bake for another 10 minutes. Let cool completely before serving.

⊰ KITCHEN MEMORIES ⊱

My daughter, Fanny, as you can well imagine, grew up in the restaurant and garden. She developed a great palate and awareness of what's important about eating delicious things and eating them in season. These principles of the restaurant have been absorbed by her, so it makes it very difficult for her to be in circumstances where that's not happening. So of course when she went to college, she couldn't possibly eat the food and it provoked me so much that I went and talked to the college president. He said that he'd be interested in my helping to do something about it. We joined forces with a group on campus called Food from the Earth that is interested in getting organic local food into the cafeterias. Now it is becoming a kind of model of how it might be done. We formed a little steering committee, and we have three people who work in our office. It's moving along. We insist that eating well is not a privilege, but a right.

Fanny didn't cook much when she was growing up, but it's quite amazing what's going on right now. She worked in the restaurant for a couple of summers, but I never knew that she was as accomplished as she is. She's been calling me and asking how to make braised chicken and puff pastry. She got an apartment off-campus so she can come home in the afternoon and cook dinner for herself and her friends. You cannot imagine! It's exactly when and how I started, so it's just fantastic.

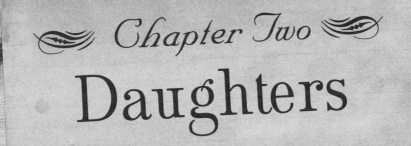

Chapter Two
Daughters

MOST OF US WHO LOVE TO COOK have fond memories of the very first time we cooked something by ourselves in our mothers' kitchens. For some it was a pivotal experience—hours, or maybe even just a few minutes, spent fumbling one's way through familiar yet strange and unknown territory to emerge with a plate brimming with food that came truly from the heart and brought pleasure to the ones we loved most. Many of the recipes included in this chapter were inspired by the chefs' first independent culinary experiences in their mothers' or grandmothers' kitchens and, like Audrey Lennon's Black Beans and Rice, have been passed down for generations. Some, like Rozanne Gold's Rustic Pear Cake, have been created for the enjoyment of their mothers, and still others, like Dorothy Hamilton's daughter's Olivia's Famous Omelet, are the efforts of tomorrow's fledgling chefs. Like the rest of the recipes in this book, they are wildly diverse and yet, somehow all familiar.

Fried Polenta
❧ *Margaret Fox* ❧

At a certain point in Margaret Fox's young life, she asked her mother, who was an ambitious and inquisitive family cook, "Can't we have something without a sauce on it?" Still awed today by her mom's ability to get beautiful meals on the table by six o'clock every night after a long day of work, Margaret says that even now, as a chef, this is something she herself has yet to accomplish. Her mother loved to experiment with new dishes and once she cooked something she would move on to the next thing. Margaret's family grew to realize that the only way for them to get her to cook the same thing twice was to tell her that it wasn't quite right the first time around. During her junior year in high school, Margaret actually dropped out of school for the year, and her mother told her that she needed to find something to do. She suggested that Margaret try her hand at making bread. She gave her a scale and an oven thermometer, showed her how to do it, and by the fifth day, Margaret was doing it on her own without the thermometer. Not long afterwards she started offering bread-baking classes at the local Unitarian church. She was just seventeen years old and the classes were a huge hit. From that time on she was always involved in cooking in one way or another—whether it was cooking coq au vin for her college French class or one hundred popovers in a tiny oven.

After college, Margaret drove up to Mendocino and literally found a job and a place to live within one hour of arriving in town. She worked in the bakery at the Mendocino Hotel for a year and a half, and then when Margaret was only twenty-five years old, she and three friends bought a little restaurant, Café Beaujolais. Margaret continued to run Café Beaujolais until 2000, when she sold it—twenty-three years after she bought it. Today Margaret is a professional consultant and the mother of eight year old Celeste, who loves to experiment in the kitchen. Her family loved breakfast, and this Fried Polenta recipe is another Fox family breakfast favorite. It is a great change of pace from traditional pancakes, waffles, and oatmeal.

SERVES 4

½ teaspoon salt
1 cup polenta meal
Cornmeal for dredging

4 tablespoons (½ stick) unsalted butter
Maple syrup or brown sugar

1 Over high heat, bring 5 cups of water to a boil, add the salt, and slowly pour in the polenta meal, stirring constantly. Turn the heat down and cook for 15 minutes, continuing to stir.

2 Pour into a lightly buttered pan. You can use a loaf pan, which was traditional in my family. My daughter likes to use a mold of several small (about 2-inch-wide) hearts usually used to make heart-shaped poached eggs. After pouring the polenta into a pan, refrigerate it until firm.

3 Slice the chilled polenta into ½-inch pieces and dredge lightly in cornmeal on both sides. Heat a 10- to 12-inch sauté pan, add about 2 tablespoons of butter, and when melted, place the polenta in the pan. Do not crowd. Cook over medium heat until golden brown and flip. Cook until browned on the other side, adding more butter if necessary.

4 Divide among plates and serve with warm maple syrup or brown sugar.

⊰ KITCHEN MEMORIES ⊱

In my house my mother had, and I'm happy to say that I now have, a classic waffle iron that probably weighs 5,000 pounds and pulls more power than the entire county of Mendocino. This waffle iron, which was kept a mile back in a cupboard, was excavated for Sunday breakfasts, which would be gatherings of cousins. It was a big deal. At no other time did we eat waffles. Everybody got such a huge kick out of these waffles—they seemed magical. So when I opened the restaurant I decided that I wanted to do all these great things that have been relegated to just special occasions. We had waffles, pancakes, French toast, coffee cake, eggs any style, great omelets, and great fruit platters. We were in this old farmhouse with wood floors and a wood stove and it was such a nurturing place. I think people thought they had died and gone to heaven.

Apple Sour Cream Coffee Cake
Kerry L. Heffernan
THE FAIRMONT HOTEL, SAN FRANCISCO

Kerry Heffernan grew up in San Gabriel Valley, California, surrounded by avocado trees and citrus groves in the 1960s and 1970s, when it was still ranchland, largely untouched by suburban sprawl. Her mother had a kitchen garden and Kerry was constantly exposed to good fresh foods. She learned to cook at her mother's side, grilling fresh fish and meats on their outdoor gas grill (a novelty at that time). Kerry and her brother ate everything—they weren't picky children who ate only macaroni and cheese.

When Kerry Heffernan, now executive sous-chef at the Fairmont Hotel in San Francisco, owned Autumn Moon Café, she would sell about twenty-five to thirty of these cakes a week, which is about 250 to 300 slices! People were crazy for it, and every time she tried to create a new coffee cake with blueberries or peaches, there would be a "near riot." Eventually she gave in and kept the cake on the menu, even during the summer months when other fruits were in season. It's a cake her mother taught her to make, and despite the clamoring of her customers, Kerry says this recipe adapts well to any type of fruit. The batter is perfect for pineapple upside-down cake as well.

MAKES ONE 10-INCH BUNDT CAKE

CAKE BATTER

1 cup (2 sticks) unsalted butter,
   at room temperature
2 cups granulated sugar
6 eggs
Zest of 2 lemons
4 cups unbleached all-purpose flour
2 teaspoons baking powder
2 teaspoons baking soda
½ teaspoon salt
2 cups sour cream

CRUMB TOPPING

½ cup light or dark brown sugar
½ cup unbleached all-purpose flour
½ teaspoon ground cinnamon
½ cup (1 stick) unsalted cold butter
¼ cup finely chopped walnuts (optional)

2 cups 1-inch-diced apples tossed in
   cinnamon sugar

1 Preheat the oven to 350° F and grease a 10-inch bundt pan.

2 Cream the butter with an electric mixer. Add the sugar and beat until light in color and fluffy. Beat in the eggs, one at a time. Add the lemon zest and beat again.

3 In a medium-sized bowl, mix together the flour, baking powder, baking soda, and salt. Add the flour mixture to the butter mixture alternately with the sour cream. Beat the batter until smooth.

4 Prepare the crumb topping: In a small bowl, combine the brown sugar, flour, and cinnamon. Cut in the butter, using a pastry cutter, until the texture is coarse. Stir in the walnuts, if using.

5 Pour half the batter into the prepared pan. Spread the apples evenly over the batter. Pour the remaining batter over the apples. Sprinkle the crumb topping evenly over the batter.

6 Bake for 70 minutes, or until a toothpick inserted in the middle comes out clean. Cool in the pan for 10 minutes, then loosen the edges with a sharp knife. Invert onto a serving plate to unmold. The crumb "topping" now becomes the bottom of the cake.

⊰ KITCHEN MEMORIES ⊱

My grandmother was a professional chef. Back in those days, when you were a professional cook you were a "domestic." She was of Italian heritage and was born in 1900. She worked in wealthy people's homes, and sometime in the 1940s she moved to Hollywood and began working for Clifton Webb. He was a pretty big movie star at the time, and she did all the cooking for him and his partner. She knew all the big movie stars. People raved about her food. She was very, very good, but back in those days they ate a lot of roasted meats. It wasn't what we would consider super-gourmet today, but it was back then. At one point he started to get a little bit of heart trouble so his doctor told him he had to cut back on cookies, cream, butter, sugar—all that stuff. She made what we would now call Mexican wedding cakes. He loved them so she kept making them in spite of the doctor's orders. She worked for him a long time and was still working for him when I was born. I think he died in '67. There are pictures of me in his backyard with him next to his swimming pool. When he passed away she moved to Palm Springs and worked for Dean Martin. She retired at age 72 in 1972.

Artichoke and Potato Salad with Licorice-Mint
❧ Gale Gand ❧
TRU, CHICAGO

Early to the "culinary" spotlight, Gale Gand (pictured with her mother, opposite), a native of Chicago, grabbed the attention of a *Life* magazine photographer, who snapped a picture of six-year-old Gale making mud pies. In that moment the photographer may have unwittingly planted the seed for culinary stardom, but Gale didn't find her way to the foodservice business for more than a decade. She started cooking in restaurants, as many chefs have, to help finance her college career. An art major, she quickly discovered that she had an affinity for the culinary arts, or more specifically, pastry arts. Before graduation she took a trip to France to learn about pastry at La Varenne cooking school and started a catering business.

Not long afterwards, while working at the Strathallen Hotel in Rochester, New York, she met her future husband and business partner. Three years later the two moved to New York City. Gale's desserts at The Gotham Bar and Grill were awarded three stars by *New York Times* critic Bryan Miller, and her career took off. Today she is an award-winning author, star of *Sweet Dreams* on the Food Network, and owner of a self-branded root beer company in addition to being executive pastry chef and partner in Chicago's famed restaurant TRU.

While her work has taken her all over the world, Gale's cooking still hearkens back to the classic American childhood favorites that evoke memories of home and Mom. At her former Chicago restaurant, Brasserie T, she served food that made you feel good just to be able to eat. A chef, pastry chef, manager, soft-drink maker, and mother of Gio (with twins on the way), Gale serves milk and cookies as a dessert, root beer floats made with her own root beer, and many more items that strike a nostalgic note. Both the potato salad and the corn bread recipes that Gale shared are reminiscent of summer family picnics and barbecues—those special moments when school is out, the weather is warm, and growing up seems very far away.

Mom's Secret Mint now is available in many different varieties, from lemon and pineapple to chocolate and licorice. You can often find these unusual varieties at a local farmers' market throughout the summer.

8 artichoke hearts, cooked and
    quartered

8 new potatoes, cooked and quartered

1 cup green beans, cut into 1-inch
    lengths and blanched

½ bulb fennel, chopped fine

5 leaves licorice-mint, julienned *(see note)*

1 shallot, minced

1 tablespoon fresh lemon juice

1 tablespoon fresh orange juice

1 tablespoon fresh lime juice

½ cup extra virgin olive oil

Salt and pepper to taste

2 tablespoons grated Parmesan

In a large bowl, toss together all of the ingredients. Serve chilled with Roasted Corn Bread (recipe follows).

Roasted Corn Bread

～ Gale Gand ～

TRU, CHICAGO

MAKES ONE 9-INCH ROUND CAKE

¾ cup all-purpose flour

2 teaspoons baking powder

3 tablespoons light or dark brown sugar

1 teaspoon salt

1¼ cups yellow cornmeal

7 ounces unsalted butter

1 cup milk

1 egg

1 ear corn, roasted under the broiler, kernels only

2 tablespoons pureed roasted garlic (see note)

1 tablespoon chopped fresh chives

1 small log goat cheese

1 Preheat oven to 400° F. Generously butter a 9-inch round cake pan.

2 In a large bowl combine the flour, baking powder, brown sugar, salt, and corn-meal. Set aside. In a small saucepan, combine the butter and milk, warming just to melt the butter.

3 In a separate bowl, whisk the egg slightly, then whisk in the warm butter-milk mixture.

4 Make a well in the center of the dry ingredients and pour in the egg-butter-milk mixture. Mix together with the roasted corn kernels, roasted garlic, and chives.

Mom's Secret Roasted garlic is a wonderfully versatile ingredient to have on hand for dressing pasta, flavoring sauces, and enriching soups and stews. Slice crosswise the top ¼ inch of a whole head of garlic, season lightly with salt and pepper, and drizzle lightly with olive oil. Place in a small pan and cover tightly with foil. Roast in a 400° oven for around 40 minutes, or until the cloves feel soft. Let cool slightly, then squeeze out each clove from its peel into a bowl. Refrigerate what you do not use immediately.

5 Pour the batter into the cake pan and bake for 20 to 25 minutes, or until a skewer inserted in the center comes out clean.

6 Serve in slices spread with goat cheese.

Hominy and Smoked Ham Risotto with Manchego Cheese

Patricia Williams

MORRELLS RESTAURANT, NEW YORK

This dish exemplifies many of the wonderful flavors and ingredients of Patricia's cultural heritage. Her Native American and Mexican culinary traditions come together in the form of Manchego cheese (a classic Spanish firm cheese), smoked ham, and hominy to create a contemporary favorite.

SERVES 10

1 or 2 smoked ham hocks, (about 3 pounds)

14 tablespoons (1¾ sticks) unsalted butter

4 cups small-diced onion (approximately 4 small onions)

2 pounds white hominy, soaked overnight

Kosher salt to taste

Freshly cracked black pepper, to taste

Manchego cheese, shaved

1 Cover ham hocks with water in a large pot. Bring to a boil over high heat, reduce heat just so it simmers, and cook for several hours, until meat falls easily from the bone. Strain liquid and add water if needed to make 1 quart. Pull bones and fat from meat and discard. Dice meat and reserve.

2 Melt 1 stick of butter over medium-high heat in a large saucepan. Add the onions and cook until caramelized. Heat the stock to a bare simmer in a large saucepan.

3 Drain the hominy and stir into the onions. Add a small amount of stock and cook on medium heat. Stir until it is absorbed. Add more stock and stir again until it is absorbed. Repeat until all the stock is gone.

4 Cook over medium-low heat until the hominy is soft, stirring so it does not stick to the bottom of the pan. Add the remaining butter, salt, and pepper.

5 Top with diced ham and shaved Manchego cheese. Serve.

Marinated Beef with Lime Sauce
❧ *Nadsa de Monteiro-Perry* ❧
ELEPHANT WALK, BOSTON AND CAMBRIDGE
CARAMBOLA, WALTHAM, MASSACHUSETTS

Daughter of Longteine de Monteiro, Nadsa de Monteiro-Perry was a natural in the kitchen at a very young age. According to Longteine, Nadsa was a quick study who "liked to do everything fast and a little bit sloppy. If she wanted to bake a cake, for example, she would drop the flour on the floor and pick up the flour and use it again. She was that kind of kid. The cook used to scream at her and say, 'You cannot do that!' and she would say, 'It's okay, I did.'" Nadsa remembers her mother cooking all the time in spite of the fact that they always had cooks. Wherever they lived Longteine would experiment with dishes native to the region—Yugoslavian food when they lived in Yugoslavia, Chinese food when they lived in Taiwan—helping Nadsa to develop a well-rounded palate very early in life.

When her family moved to France, Nadsa went to Paris where she reconnected with and eventually wed her high school sweetheart, Bob Perry. Two years later Nadsa became a naturalized American citizen, and the couple moved to the United States. In 1989 they brought Nadsa's parents over to live with them. Not long afterwards Nadsa's sister and brother-in-law joined them there, and they all lived cheek by jowl in the small Perry household for a year. With money from the sale of their restaurant in France, the de Monteiros opened the first Elephant Walk, a French-Cambodian restaurant in Somerville, Massachusetts. The whole family, except Nadsa, who was working as a travel agent at the time, worked there, and it was an instant success. Nadsa would come home every evening to an empty house and found herself feeling lonely. Before long she began hanging around the restaurant, waiting tables and hostessing. One day, when the French cook didn't show up for work Nadsa was prodded by her family to take a spot on the line—and she loved it! Eventually she quit her day job altogether to join the rest of her family at the restaurant. Within two years Nadsa became head chef of the second Elephant's Walk, on Beacon Street in Boston. She earned three-star reviews and quickly opened another restaurant, Carambola, in Waltham, Massachusetts. Today Nadsa and her family run three restaurants. This is one of the recipes Nadsa cooked in Paris when she became homesick for her mother's cooking.

7 cloves garlic, finely chopped

3 tablespoons mushroom soy sauce

2 tablespoons sugar

¼ teaspoon salt

Freshly ground black pepper

1½ pounds flank steak or boneless
sirloin, cut into 1-inch cubes

2 tablespoons vegetable oil

1 head green leaf lettuce, leaves
separated, washed, and drained

2 tablespoons fresh lime juice

1 teaspoon water

½ teaspoon freshly ground black pepper

1 To make the marinade, combine the garlic, soy sauce, sugar, salt, and pepper in a large bowl. Add the beef and stir to coat. Set aside for 20 to 30 minutes.

2 In a large skillet, heat the oil over high heat. Sauté the beef for 3 to 4 minutes, browning on all sides, until medium-rare. Arrange the lettuce leaves on a platter and place the beef cubes on top.

3 Combine the lime juice, water, and pepper in a small bowl and serve with the beef as a dipping sauce.

⊰ KITCHEN MEMORIES ⊱

When we went to France, I moved away from my parents for the first time. My mother had, by then, a restaurant in the south of France, and I lived in Paris and was hungering for some real Cambodian food because there were a lot of Chinese and Vietnamese restaurants, but there weren't really any authentic Cambodian restaurants. So I'd crave one food or another and I'd call my mom up and say, "I'm craving such and such a thing, will you give me the recipe?" She would say, "Well, sure, you put some of this and some of that and a little bit of this and a little bit of that," and I'd say, "Well, how much?" She'd say, "Well, you know, enough," and that's when I started to cook. I was always able to recreate things almost perfectly and I learned to use my taste buds to say this is what I remember because this is exactly what I was craving.

Walleye Baked with Hazelnuts and Sage
❧ *Lucia Watson* ❧
LUCIA'S RESTAURANT & WINE BAR, MINNEAPOLIS

Lucia Watson (pictured with her parents, opposite) is one of the lucky ones—she has always known what her career would be. It never occurred to her to be anything but a chef. Her first restaurant experience was at L'Auberge, a tiny French bistro near Washington, D.C., in Middleburg, Virginia. She was waiting tables just to make money but really wanted to be in the kitchen, so she started pestering the chef to let her help him. It took a while, but he finally caved and told her she could do some prep. She still remembers her first job there—she had to peel a case of baby artichokes. Lucia immediately "loved the insane feeling of the professional kitchen, the creativity, energy, and pace around food."

After working in Washington, D.C., she returned to her home state of Minnesota and lied about her experience to get a job left vacant by the pastry chef the very day she interviewed. The head chef was a tall, imposing Austrian man with a goatee "who spit on you when he talked," but who taught her a great deal after she managed to muddle through her first months in the pastry department. From there she started and ran a successful catering business but decided to move on and open her own restaurant instead of investing in more equipment and large vans for the catering business. That original thirty-two-seat restaurant has grown to become what is now Lucia's Restaurant & Wine Bar.

Her love of food and cooking was, without a doubt, inspired by her upbringing. Anyone who grew up in a family in which you started talking about what you were going to eat for dinner as you were cleaning up the lunch dishes would feel right at home at Lucia Watson's family table. With a homemaker mom and a father in the grocery business, Lucia's family life literally revolved around food.

She likes to serve this walleye dish, which hearkens back to those childhood summers on Lake Raney, where the water remains ice cold even in summer. Aficionados say fish from cold waters always tastes fresher. Catfish, trout, or any firm, white fish can be substituted. Lucia recommends serving it with baked acorn squash and wild rice.

SERVES 2

2 cleaned, fresh walleye fillets
2 tablespoons butter, plus a little
  more to grease the cookie sheet
Salt and pepper to taste
2 tablespoons chopped fresh sage
1 lemon, halved
2 tablespoons toasted and lightly
  chopped hazelnuts

1 Preheat the oven to 375° F.
If necessary, rinse the fish in
ice-cold water and pat dry with
paper towels.

FATHERS & DAUGHTERS

2 Lightly grease a cookie sheet.
Lay the fish on the cookie sheet and sprinkle with the salt
and pepper. Bake the fish in the oven for about 10 to 15 minutes, or until the
flesh is opaque and very tender when you peek inside.

3 Meanwhile, melt the butter. Just before the fish is done baking, add the sage
to the butter with a squeeze of fresh lemon juice. Spoon the butter and sage over
the fish and sprinkle the hazelnuts on top.

❧ KITCHEN MEMORIES ❧

Some of my most influential food memories come from the time I spent at my
family's cabin on an island in Lake Raney at the border of Minnesota and
Ontario, Canada. The island is extremely isolated and the only way to get sup-
plies is by boat. During my childhood there was no electricity and all the family
had to keep the food fresh was an icehouse, so there was a lot of planning and
frugality involved in a trip to the lake. The island is 300 acres and there was no
entertainment, so food and cooking were a huge part of our lives every summer.
  My grandmother is the most influential person in my cooking life. She and
I would pick blueberries and catch fish, and when we began to run out of sup-
plies, my grandmother would amaze me by cooking wholesome, flavorful meals
on a single woodstove with very few ingredients.

Pan-Roasted Striped Bass with Butter, Fresh Herbs, and Lemon
Jody Adams
RIALTO, CAMBRIDGE, MASSACHUSETTS ❖ BLU, BOSTON

Jody says that her family is as WASPy as they come, yet her mother was an adventurous cook, not at all afraid to try out recipes in Julia Child's or Elizabeth David's books. Their Providence, Rhode Island, neighborhood was primarily Portuguese and Italian, and Jody's mom was constantly bringing home new things to try out. Jody distinctly remembers the day she brought fennel home—nobody liked it, but her mother persevered and continued to bring home new and unusual ingredients. Her family never went out to dinner unless they were traveling—Yankees through and through, they didn't see a reason to pay someone to cook for them when they could make perfectly good food at home. Jody, on the other hand, loved restaurants and eating out.

Her first foray into the world of food was during high school at a local cooking school, where a neighbor was teaching some classes. The neighbor thought Jody might like to earn some extra money washing dishes for the cooking school. Jody realized early on that it would be easier to manage the job if she were allowed to wash dishes as the classes were being taught. As a bonus she learned a lot about cooking through, as she puts it, "osmosis and general interest." The course, based on Madeline Kamman's curriculum, had a solid foundation in French and Italian cuisine, and it inspired Jody to take another job at a local gourmet food company. Soon afterward she began looking for her first restaurant job and decided to pursue employment with Lydia Shire in Boston. Gordon Hammersley was the sous chef there, and when he left to open Hammersley's in Boston, Jody joined him and worked there for three years before taking a job as chef at Michela's, also in Boston.

Currently the executive chef/owner of Rialto and blu, Jody has two children, the younger of whom was born just around the time Rialto was making its debut. An award-winning chef by day, Jody is just another member of the family at home and thoroughly enjoys not being in charge of her home kitchen. She loves to let her husband take over or have the kids, Oliver and Roxanne, give her directions during family meal preparations. This recipe is Jody's own, but its inspiration is the summer family meals of her childhood.

2 tablespoons vegetable oil

4 (6-ounce) pieces striped bass, skin on

Kosher salt and freshly ground black pepper to taste

¼ cup chopped fresh herbs such as basil, parsley, tarragon, and chives (or, as Mom says, "whatever suits your fancy.")

4 tablespoons (½ stick) unsalted butter, cut into 8 slices

Juice of ½ lemon

1 Heat the oil in a large cast-iron pan over medium-high heat. Season the fish all over with salt and pepper. Add the fish, skin side down to the pan. Sprinkle the fish with the herbs, and put 2 slices of butter on each fish.

2 Cover, reduce the heat to medium-low, and cook until done, about 15 minutes. Baste the fish several times with butter during the cooking.

3 Transfer the fish to four warm plates. Add the lemon juice to the pan with the butter, swirl, season the pan sauce with salt and pepper, and pour over the fish. Serve immediately.

⊰ KITCHEN MEMORIES ⊱

I was shocked in 1984 when Congress implemented a much-needed moratorium on fishing for striped bass . I was all for protecting the stocks, but it left a huge hole in our summer table. Striped bass, with blue fish, were our fish—they came from the waters we swam in on the Cape. My father caught and cleaned them, my mother cooked them, and we all ate them with corn and tomatoes in August—tasting best, of course, when it all happened right on the beach with clusters of friends around. Fortunately, the fisheries management plan worked, and striped bass is now back on our table.

This dish ties my childhood family together. I've been a professional cook for twenty years, and I've learned many fancy techniques, but more importantly, I've learned to allow the true characteristic of an ingredient to shine. In this striped-bass recipe, I haven't moved very far from my mother's simple treatment of salt, pepper and lemon—I'm back where I started.

In the summer we're often together on the Cape, and we cook while my parents relax. We light up the grill outside and we get striped bass or bluefish and go to the farmer's stand and get tomatoes and corn, eggplant, cucumbers, and fresh herbs. It's very Italian in style, just like my mother's earliest cooking.

Olivia's Famous Omelet
Dorothy Hamilton
THE FRENCH CULINARY INSTITUTE, NEW YORK

Dorothy Hamilton went to college in England, and the food there was absolutely inedible. Fortunately for her, she lived in a dormitory with a group of French girls who felt the same way and had access to a kitchenette. They taught her to make vinaigrette, introduced her to her first yogurt, and fed her all sorts of delightful cheeses. During holidays when she wasn't going back to the United States, she would take trips to France, which is where she fell in love with French cooking.

After college she joined the Peace Corps and was stationed in Bangkok, Thailand, where for three years she ate in the same restaurant every night. Just before her scheduled return to the U.S., she asked the owner of the restaurant for all the recipes to take back with her. The recipes were not documented, so instead Dorothy was invited to work in the restaurant, which she did. To this day that is the sum total of her professional cooking life—except for the fact that she's currently the president of New York City's French Culinary Institute.

When she returned from Thailand, the U.S. was in a recession and the job market was terrible. With little training and no foreseeable prospects, she took a receptionist job at Apex Technical School, which her father owned. She discovered that she really enjoyed working with the students and over the years worked her way up to president of the entire school. She was invited on a trip to visit the top European technical schools at that point. On that trip she discovered the official cooking school of Paris and decided that she needed to convince her father that in addition to a welding school and an air-conditioning school, Apex needed to have a cooking school because she "had sort of this romantic notion that some day I'd like to open a French restaurant because it was reminiscent of my European experience." Luckily her father was quite indulgent and allowed her to start the French Culinary Institute, even financing it during the early years. Dorothy and her father struck an agreement with the French government to bring the chefs and the curriculum from France. Today it has been Americanized to a certain degree, but it's largely the same as the program in the Paris school.

Dorothy's daughter, Olivia, now eleven years old, has grown up surrounded by chefs and loves the world of food. The following two recipes are hers.

⊰ KITCHEN MEMORIES ⊱

Olivia was literally baptized into the food profession. When *Food Arts* magazine had its tenth anniversary, its staff did a crossing on the *QEII* and they asked the French Culinary Institute to be part of it. Olivia was six months old and was getting baptized in England because we were married there, so we brought her on the *QEII* with us. Her first public debut was in the pages of *Food Arts*.

When she was in kindergarten, the teacher put together a cookbook from the kids, and each kid had to describe what he or she was going to cook. One kid said, "To cook pizza you have to get ten pounds of flour, two tomatoes, a bowl of cheese and then you make the oven as hot as the sun and you put it in there for three hours. . ." It's really cute. Most kids talked about pizza. Some said challah bread, and some recipes were about how to make potato latkes, so it was a real indication of where they came from. When it got to Olivia's it said, "Olivia and Mom's Ten-Layer Cake," which I never remember making with her, but I used to make layer cakes all the time with her. I wanted something incredibly simple to do because she is a very controlling person and she'd never want me to show her how to do anything, so I used to buy the Duncan Hines cakes because they have the pictures on the back. From the time she was four she really felt like she was making them. So for the kindergarten cookbook she said, "Olivia and Mom's Ten-Layer Cake. Get the flour, put the eggs in the flour, add the water and oil. Grease the pans. Whisk together very fine." It reads like a real recipe. She had a great sense of cooking and procedure from a very early age.

SERVES 1

2 eggs	Pinch salt
1 teaspoon milk	1 tablespoon truffle butter

1 Crack the eggs in a bowl, add the milk, a pinch of salt, and beat vigorously with a fork.

2 Brown the truffle butter in a small sauté pan, taking care not to burn it.

3 Pour the eggs into the pan and cook until the eggs are partially set, then flip them over. Cook until lightly browned.

Cuban Black Beans and Rice
❧ *Audrey Lennon* ❧

Recently accepted to Les Amis d'Escoffiers Society, Audrey Lennon (pictured with her mother, below) didn't go to cooking school until she was in her forties. In fact, she wasn't doing any professional cooking at all before then. For eleven years she was a mother and housewife, cooking for PTA meetings and events like any other mother would, and as her three sons grew, she took a job in communications. Later still she worked as a contractor renovating brownstones in New York City and even became involved in international finance for a short time before deciding to attend the Mid-Florida Tech culinary program to learn about catering.

At the top of the game even as an inexperienced recent graduate, she entered her first cooking competition, walked away with a gold medal, and took a job at one of the largest caterers in her area. In a joint venture with Lew Gardens, she worked with clients like AT&T, Disney, and two city mayors. Her business grew rapidly and Audrey kept up, in spite of five hip replacements, but after the final surgery her doctor told her that she could "play in the kitchen, not stay in the kitchen." She created a culinary program for kids at the Boys and Girls Club—not only did she manage to get seventeen-year-old boys to put napkins on their laps before a meal, but three of her students were recently awarded scholarships to the Cordon Bleu school. Currently Audrey is working with the Boys and Girls Club to create a cookie they can market to help with fund-raising. She has also recently launched Sauceress, her own line of soups, sauces, and spices.

Audrey Lennon's heritage alone—Spanish-speaking grandparents from the

West Indies who spent a number of years living in Cuba on her mother's side, and Native American and Creole on her father's side—makes for an interesting culinary adventure. One of the dishes Audrey most associates with her childhood is Black Beans and Rice.

1 (8-ounce) package yellow rice mix	¼ cup sherry, plus additional to garnish
1 onion, chopped	½ teaspoon dried basil
1 green bell pepper, chopped	¼ teaspoon dried thyme
1 celery stalk, chopped	¼ teaspoon ground cumin
1 carrot, chopped	¼ teaspoon dried sage
2 tablespoons olive oil	Dash ground allspice
2 teaspoons chopped garlic	½ teaspoon salt
2 cups canned black beans, undrained	½ teaspoon pepper
½ cup cooked ham or smoked turkey, diced	1 teaspoon Cajun seasoning
	Tomato wedges, for garnish
1 cup chicken broth	Fresh parsley, for garnish

1   Preheat the oven to 350° F. Bring 2 cups of water to a boil in a large saucepan. Stir in rice, cover, and reduce heat to a simmer. After 15 minutes, remove from heat and let rest while you prepare the beans.

2   Sauté onion, green pepper, celery, and carrot in oil over medium heat until soft. Add the garlic as the vegetables begin to soften.

3   Combine all of the remaining ingredients, except the garnishes, in a saucepan. Bring to a boil and simmer, uncovered, for 30 minutes, or until the black beans are tender and the liquid has been reduced by one-half.

4   Mix with 2 cups of the partially cooked rice. Place in an 8 x 12" casserole dish. Cover and bake for 20 minutes, or until the liquid is absorbed. Garnish with tomato wedges and parsley and serve. For extra flavor, sprinkle a few dashes of sherry over the cooked dish.

⊰ KITCHEN MEMORIES ⊱

This is a basic West Indian dish that I learned to do very young. Once I was doing a public demo with this. A Cuban couple had some and came back with ten people, including this sweet little old lady. She had a sample, looked up at me, and tears came to her eyes. I said, "What's the matter, it's not too hot, is it?" She told me it tasted just like her grandmother's recipe that she'd lost years ago.

Potted Quail with Creamy Southern Grits
❧ *Eve Felder* ❧

THE CULINARY INSTITUTE OF AMERICA, HYDE PARK, NEW YORK

Raised in Charleston, South Carolina, Eve Felder (pictured below) grew up surrounded by ocean and farmland with a mother who loved to cook and a father who thoroughly enjoyed the bounty of the land and sea around him. He was an avid hunter and fisherman, and both activities affected Eve's relationship with food. As a little girl, she helped her mother cook family meals of freshly caught fish or game birds for traditional southern dinners that were served promptly at 2 P.M. In adolescence she enjoyed fishing, shrimping, and crabbing with her friends on the delta, where they would gather to cook their catch over an open fire. In spite of Eve's obvious passion for cooking, her parents had no aspirations for her to become a chef. It just wasn't an option for a southern girl—she was expected to become a lovely wife and southern belle. They urged her to go to college, and she did.

After college Eve began working in restaurants and developed an interest in organic farming, which led her to move to Omaha, Nebraska, with her best friend, where they took a stab at starting an organic garden. They replanted twice before they realized that the soil was so polluted, nothing but corn would grow there.

Not long after her failed farming venture, Eve was working as a chef in a 100-seat restaurant in Omaha and was researching menus when she came across a reference to Lindsay Shere and Alice Waters. She was thrilled to find that someone out there was doing what she wanted to do, but thought she needed an education before she could join them. She applied to The Culinary Institute of America (CIA) with the sole intention of eventually having Alice Waters as a mentor. As soon as she started school she wrote Alice a "love letter" and was offered an externship, and then a job. Starting out in charge of washing lettuces and making pasta, Eve worked her way up to chef of Chez Panisse and stayed for seven years before returning to the CIA as a chef-instructor. Today she is Associate Dean of Culinary Arts and oversees the culinary program.

One of Eve's favorite meals in childhood was quail with grits. Another was shrimp with grits, which she still cooks every time she returns home to South Carolina.

SERVES 8

8 quails, bone-in
2 teaspoons salt
1 teaspoon pepper
1 cup all-purpose flour

1 cup bacon fat
1 cup onion, diced small
3 cups chicken stock

1 Season the birds with salt and pepper. Dredge in flour to coat lightly; pat off the excess flour so it doesn't burn in the fat.

2 Heat a cast-iron pan and add the bacon fat. When it is hot, brown the birds over moderate heat until golden. Remove from the pan and reserve.

3 Add the diced onion and cook until translucent.

4 Place the quail back in the pan and add enough chicken stock to cover by two-thirds. Partially cover the pan.

5 Cook for 1 hour until the quail are tender and the gravy is thickened. Serve with grits for a fall or winter breakfast or supper.

Mom's Secret This recipe can be used for doves or marsh hens. We called this "boggy" when I was growing up because it was as if the birds were cooking in a bog—half submerged in the murky bubbling sauce. Of course, our birds always had a little shot in them from my father's gun but we spat that out. This is an old fashioned recipe and some people may think the birds are overcooked but it really is a traditional and delicious southern recipe.

CREAMY SOUTHERN GRITS

SERVES 4

1½ teaspoons salt (more if needed)
⅔ cup grits

1½ cups milk (more if needed)
2 tablespoons unsalted butter

1 Combine 3 cups of water and the salt in a heavy-bottomed pot. Bring to a boil.

2 Slowly whisk in the grits so as to avoid lumps. As they thicken add the milk in ½-cup increments until 1 cup has been used. At this point the grits should be able to sustain a slow continual simmer. Cover with a lid.

3 After 30 minutes add the remaining ½ cup of milk and continue to cook. The secret to excellent grits is a slow, long simmer with the pan covered. They may be cooked for a minimum of an hour up to 3 hours. Adjust the milk to maintain a creamy consistency.

4 Place the grits on individual plates and put a pat of butter in the center. This will melt and form a luscious pool. It may be stirred in by the person eating it or eaten alone with a little spoon (if you are four years old), or you can even make a thin stream with a fork from the pool of butter and take small bites as the butter dribbles down the side of the mound of grits.

⊰ KITCHEN MEMORIES ⊱

I have childhood memories of my father bringing home fish and ducks and marsh hens. I have vivid memories of the smell of a wet duck as we pulled off the feathers and then opened up the cavity to remove the insides. There's an intimate relationship with food when you get it out of its environment and follow it all the way through the cooking process. During my adolescence my father had a duck-hunting club, and it was a rickety shack with no running water and no electricity. Daddy would use it in the fall and winter to hunt, and in the spring and summer we would use it as our weekend place. We would collect rainwater and take showers outside, and we had propane to light gas lights. I was brought up fishing and pulling crab traps. And shrimp! We could stand on the dyke and throw a cast net and catch a hundred pounds of shrimp in a half-hour.

Rustic Pear Cake
✑ *Rozanne Gold* ✑

Rozanne Gold, once the chef for former New York City Mayor Ed Koch, says this cake is "so easy to make that it almost makes itself!" It can be made in one bowl only and is truly a cake of simple pleasures. It's something she often makes for her mother (pictured with Rozanne below). Rozanne recommends eating it with a cup of tea or a chilled glass of sweet Tokay wine in honor of her mother's Hungarian roots.

SERVES 6 OR MORE

2 extra-large eggs

¼ cup milk

⅓ cup good-quality olive oil

1 tablespoon freshly grated lemon zest

⅔ cup plus 1 tablespoon sugar

1½ cups self-rising flour

4 large ripe pears (about 2 pounds)

1 Preheat the oven to 375° F. Lightly oil and flour a 9 x 1½-inch round cake pan.

2 In a large bowl, whisk together the eggs, milk, olive oil, and lemon zest. Whisk thoroughly.

3 Add ⅔ cup sugar and blend well. Stir in the flour and mix until a smooth batter is formed.

4 Peel the pears, using a small, sharp knife. Cut each pear into quarters lengthwise. Remove the tough core and seeds. Slice each quarter crosswise into ¼-inch slices. Add to the batter and stir gently to incorporate the pears completely.

5 Pour the batter into the prepared pan. Sprinkle the top with the remaining tablespoon of sugar. Bake for 50 minutes or until just firm to the touch. Remove from the oven. Cool completely before serving.

Yellow Vanilla Pound Cake
❧ *Edna Lewis* ❧

Edna grew up in Freetown, Virginia, a town founded by her grandfather, a freed slave, and went on to become the first female chef in New York City in 1946. She is an impassioned woman who not only became an acclaimed chef and African-American culinary historian, but somehow found the time and energy to adopt six Masai and Ethiopian children as well.

Edna has been instrumental in preserving the traditions of southern cooking. She is also an advocate of organic fresh produce and natural foods and believes that her passion for cooking and her love of fresh, flavorful ingredients stem from memories of her early years in Freetown. There she was surrounded by women who shared the experience of cooking in a way that demonstrated the very essence of a woman's unique ability to love and nurture her friends and family through food.

Flavor is what Edna stresses most in her cooking. Edna's family liked this recipe for its "keeping quality" and the availability of its ingredients. One need not go far from home for butter, eggs, flour, sugar, and flavoring. This cake makes a great addition to any picnic. Or enjoy it at home, warm and topped with some freshly made ice cream.

❧ KITCHEN MEMORIES ❧

I remember growing up in a little settlement, and it was like one big family. The housewives all loved to cook! If one of them made a great pie, she would pass it around. Either she'd bring it and give everybody a slice, or you went to her house to taste it. I grew up around people who were obsessed with food! The food tasted so different from how it does today; it really had a great flavor.

With cakes all the grownups had their own way of measuring, be it on a dime, nickel, teacup, or sifter, and they were perfect. It was my dream to make a pound cake to equal theirs. I learned that the formula for a good pound cake is a slow oven, cold butter, carefully measured flour (too much flour will cause the cake to crack on top), and proper mixing of butter, sugar, and eggs.

2 sticks unsalted butter, cold
1⅔ cups sugar
¼ teaspoon salt
5 medium to large eggs (not jumbo)

2 cups unbleached flour, sifted
1 tablespoon vanilla extract
1 teaspoon freshly squeezed lemon juice

1 Preheat the oven to 300° F. Butter and flour the bottom only of a 9-inch tube pan.

2 Put the butter in a large mixing bowl and work it with a wooden spoon until it becomes shiny, about 5 minutes. Add the sugar and salt and continue to work together. When well mixed, begin to stir in a circular motion until the mixture loses most of its gritty feeling. The addition of eggs will dissolve the rest.

3 Add the eggs one at a time, stirring well after each addition. After the third egg has been incorporated, add 2 tablespoons of flour and stir well. This will keep the batter from separating. Add the fourth and fifth egg and continue to stir, then add the rest of the flour in four parts, stirring well after each addition.

4 Beat in the vanilla and lemon juice.

5 Spoon the batter into the prepared pan. Place in the oven.

6 Bake for 40 minutes, then raise the temperature to 325° F for 20 minutes. Remove from the oven, run a knife around the sides of the pan, turn out right away on a wire rack, and turn face up. Cool, uncovered, for 15 minutes, then cover with a clean towel; otherwise the cake will become dry and hard.

7 When cold, store in a clean tin. Plastic containers develop an undesirable odor.

Note: Two teaspoons of almond extract can be used in place of lemon and vanilla.

Marie Brizard Cacao Nut Torte
❧ *Katy Keck* ❧
THE NEW WORLD GRILL, NEW YORK

Katy Keck's mother diligently noted in her baby book that during the first three months of her life, "Katy had no trouble" eating. "She likes food." However, little Katy didn't "care much for sleep." With no need for sleep and a love of food, Katy was, perhaps, born to be a chef.

Before she came to that realization, however, she earned her MBA and worked on Wall Street for eight years. The 1980s on Wall Street was a heady time, filled with cocktail parties and entertaining, and Katy was doing her fair share when it suddenly occurred to her that she was happier entertaining than she was at her Wall Street job. She wrote a business plan for a retail food store that was not at all well received by her colleagues at Merrill Lynch because even with her impressive margins (which she concedes were probably erroneously derived), the foodservice business just didn't offer the kinds of profits they were accustomed to reaping in business.

Instead, she set her sights on winning an apprenticeship in France. Her success led her to quit her day job and move to France for a year, where she worked in four restaurants before returning to the United States to open the New World Grill in New York City in 1993.

Today Katy is a consulting chef for New World as well as a spokesperson for Bush's Variety Beans (no, she has nothing to do with the dog!) and a participant in Windjammer's Culinary Cruises. Katy doesn't believe that her southern Indiana roots were particularly inspirational, but her mother and grandmothers were. She fondly remembers her mother's love of entertaining, her maternal grandmother's beautiful birthday cakes and elegant sherry-spiked lobster bisque, as well as her German grandmother Lena Keck's utilitarian "vats of soup and chili." This torte was inspired by a recipe of her grandmother's called Chocolate Repleven, and it helped Katy win the apprenticeship in France.

TORTE

3 whole eggs
4 egg yolks
1½ cups granulated sugar
¾ cup Marie Brizard cacao liqueur
3 cups finely ground chocolate wafer crumbs
2 teaspoons baking powder
½ teaspoon salt
2 ounces sweet chocolate
¾ cup chopped pecans

VANILLA CUSTARD SAUCE

2 cups heavy cream
1 vanilla bean, whole
4 egg yolks
4 tablespoons superfine sugar

GARNISH

½ cup confectioners' sugar
12 fresh strawberries
12 sprigs fresh mint

1 Preheat the oven to 325° F. Butter a 10-inch false-bottom tart pan and set aside.

2 Combine the whole eggs, egg yolks, and sugar. Stir in the liqueur. Add the chocolate wafer crumbs, baking powder, and salt, stirring with a wooden spoon until incorporated.

3 In the bowl of a food processor, pulse the chocolate with a steel blade until small chunks remain. Mix with the chopped pecans and stir into the torte mixture.

4 Pour into the prepared tart pan and bake for 1 hour. When properly cooked, the outer surface should appear crusty, but a toothpick inserted in the center will come out moist. Cool slightly and dust with confectioners' sugar.

5 For the custard, heat the cream in a saucepan. Split the vanilla bean lengthwise, and scrape the seeds out into the cream as you heat it. Add the whole bean to the cream and bring to a boil.

6 Beat the egg yolks and sugar in a bowl. Pour in the hot cream and whisk vigorously.

7 Return to the saucepan and place over low heat, stirring constantly, until the custard coats a wooden spoon.

8 Remove from the heat. Strain the sauce. Press a piece of plastic wrap to the surface of the custard and store in the refrigerator until serving.

9 To serve, slice the strawberries from tip to stem ends without cutting all the way through. Place a piece of torte in the center of each plate and spoon some custard on the side. Fan a strawberry and place it at the edge of the custard. Garnish with a sprig of fresh mint. Both the torte and the sauce can be prepared a day ahead.

Chapter Three
Families

WHETHER IT'S SUNDAY DINNER, a quick breakfast, a packed lunch, or a backyard barbecue, there are memories in the making in every meal we cook for our families. In this chapter the women share their favorite family recipes and the colorful stories that accompany them.

We especially enjoyed hearing about Maureen Pothier's colorful family tradition of making the extraordinary and delicious Râpé Pie and could feel the comfort Anne Willan's family derives from their favorite Butter Roast Chicken. Dina Altieri's grandmother's light and flavorful Manicotti is sure to become a favorite of countless families around the country now that we've had the privilege of sharing it with the world, and Sara Moulton's Smoked Salmon and Salmon Roe on Crispy Potato Pancakes with Horseradish Cream and Pickled Onions reminds us that something can be a family favorite, even if not everyone eats it in quite the same way.

Smoked Salmon and Salmon Roe on Crispy Potato Pancakes with Horseradish Cream and Pickled Onions

Sara Moulton

GOURMET MAGAZINE, NEW YORK

Sara Moulton didn't always know she wanted to be a chef, but after she graduated from her New York City high school and moved to Michigan to attend college, she started taking some cooking jobs while searching for her true calling. She pursued several career options but nothing worked for her. Her mother was back home in New York watching as her normally ebullient and tirelessly energetic daughter floundered, and she decided to take matters into her own hands. She wrote letters to Craig Claiborne asking what her daughter should do if she wanted to pursue a career in food. Craig told her that Sara should either go to The Culinary Institute of America or travel to Europe. The latter was too scary for Sara, so she applied to the CIA and got in. Sara just couldn't absorb enough knowledge while she was there. She was awestruck by the passion everyone had for what they were doing.

After graduation in 1977, she worked in Boston-area restaurants for the next seven years, including Harvest, with Lydia Shire, and a catering operation where she worked behind the scenes for Julia Child's cooking show. Later, she and her husband Bill moved to New York City, where she took a job as sous-chef at the three-star La Tulipe. It was her last restaurant job because she felt she was "getting old" and needed to focus on starting a family. In order to spend more time with her children Sam and

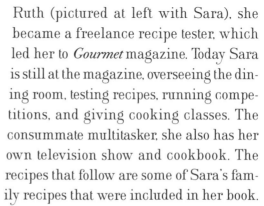

Ruth (pictured at left with Sara), she became a freelance recipe tester, which led her to *Gourmet* magazine. Today Sara is still at the magazine, overseeing the dining room, testing recipes, running competitions, and giving cooking classes. The consummate multitasker, she also has her own television show and cookbook. The recipes that follow are some of Sara's family recipes that were included in her book.

1 large baking potato

2 tablespoons unsalted butter

2 tablespoons vegetable oil

Kosher salt to taste

½ cup crème fraîche

1 tablespoon fresh lemon juice

1 tablespoon grated fresh, or drained bottled, horseradish

Freshly ground black pepper to taste

2 ounces smoked salmon, julienned

1 tablespoon caviar or salmon roe

½ cup pickled onions (see recipe page 206)

1 Peel and coarsely grate the potato. Working in batches, heat 2 teaspoons of the butter with 2 teaspoons of the vegetable oil in a large nonstick skillet over medium-high heat until very hot. Sprinkle 2 tablespoons of the potatoes into the pan, pressing into a 3-inch diameter with a spatula to create lacy, flat rounds of potatoes. Don't be concerned if you can see the bottom of the pan through gaps in the potatoes. Cook until well browned, pressing down firmly, 5 to 7 minutes per side. Season with salt while hot. (The cakes can be made several hours in advance and crisped in a hot oven before serving.)

2 Combine the crème fraîche, lemon juice, and horseradish in a small bowl and season with salt and pepper. Arrange 2 pancakes per serving on small plates. Top the pancakes with equal amounts of smoked salmon, a spoonful of horseradish cream, and a spoonful of caviar. Top with a few pickled onions and serve.

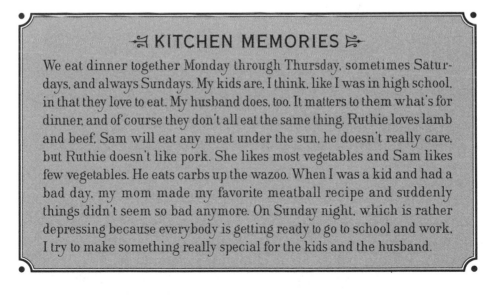

⊰ KITCHEN MEMORIES ⊱

We eat dinner together Monday through Thursday, sometimes Saturdays, and always Sundays. My kids are, I think, like I was in high school, in that they love to eat. My husband does, too. It matters to them what's for dinner, and of course they don't all eat the same thing. Ruthie loves lamb and beef. Sam will eat any meat under the sun, he doesn't really care, but Ruthie doesn't like pork. She likes most vegetables and Sam likes few vegetables. He eats carbs up the wazoo. When I was a kid and had a bad day, my mom made my favorite meatball recipe and suddenly things didn't seem so bad anymore. On Sunday night, which is rather depressing because everybody is getting ready to go to school and work, I try to make something really special for the kids and the husband.

Herbed Spaetzle
≈ Sara Moulton ≈
GOURMET MAGAZINE, NEW YORK

Sara Moulton has always loved to eat, but she wasn't always particularly picky about what she ate. In fact, she says that until she was about nine or ten, if left to her own devices all she would have eaten was hot dogs. Like most children she loved sweets and was a self-described "little butterball." Then at some point in her pre-adolescence she started eating everything. Her son, however, has a more developed taste; spaetzle is one of his favorite foods. He likes it even better when Sara sautés it and it gets nice and crispy. Sara says, "We all love spaetzle. We're a big gravy family, and you just have to have gravy or sauce with spaetzle!"

SERVES 4 TO 6

2 cups sifted all-purpose flour
1 teaspoon kosher salt
Pinch freshly ground nutmeg
2 large eggs, lightly beaten
2 tablespoons unsalted butter

2 tablespoons vegetable oil
2 tablespoons snipped fresh chives
Additional kosher salt and freshly
   ground black pepper to taste

1 Combine the flour, salt, and nutmeg in a large bowl and stir well. Whisk together the eggs and ⅔ cup of water and add to the flour mixture, beating until just smooth. The texture should be the consistency of thick pancake batter. If it's too thick, whisk in 2 to 3 tablespoons more water.

2 Drop the mixture through a spaetzle maker *(see note)* into a large pot of salted boiling water. Simmer until tender, 3 to 4 minutes. Drain and rinse under cold running water. (Spaetzle may be made a day in advance. Keep covered and chilled.)

3 Heat the butter and oil in a large skillet over high heat until hot. Add the spaetzle and cook, stirring often, until lightly browned and heated through, about 5 minutes. Add the chives and season with salt and pepper.

Mom's Secret Spaetzle can be made a day or two ahead of time. Just boil it, drain it, and put it in plastic bags. When it's time to reheat it, drop it in boiling water for a few seconds or sauté it until crispy.

When making spaetzle you can push the batter through a slotted spoon or colander, or better yet, purchase a spaetzle maker at a culinary gadget shop. It's a great tool to have on hand because spaetzle can be made quickly at the last minute.

Gravy (Meat Sauce)
Dina Altieri

NEW ENGLAND CULINARY INSTITUTE, ESSEX JUNCTION, VERMONT

Real Italians call this meat sauce "gravy." With a Sicilian mother and a father with roots in Naples, the Altieri family certainly called it gravy. Gravy and its accompanying meats are traditionally served with pasta.

MAKES 2 1/2 QUARTS

2 tablespoons extra virgin olive oil
1 pound hot or sweet Italian sausage
1 pound pork ribs, country style
1 medium onion, diced small
4 cloves garlic, minced
2 tablespoons dried basil
2 tablespoons dried Italian parsley
1 tablespoon dried oregano
1 (28-ounce) can crushed tomatoes
1 (15-ounce) can tomato sauce
1 (12-ounce) can tomato paste
Salt and pepper to taste

MEATBALLS (8 TO 10)
½ pound ground veal or beef
½ pound ground pork
1 egg
2 tablespoons bread crumbs
2 tablespoons grated Parmesan cheese
1 clove garlic, minced
2 tablespoons chopped fresh Italian parsley
Salt and black pepper to taste

1 In a 4-quart saucepan, heat the olive oil over medium heat. Add the sausage and ribs and brown evenly on all sides. Take out the meat and reserve.

2 Sweat the onion in the fat from the browned meat; add the garlic after the onion is translucent. Add the spices, tomato products, 2 cups of water, and reserved meat. Season to taste with salt and pepper and let simmer for 30 minutes.

3 Combine the ground meats, egg, bread crumbs, Parmesan, garlic, parsley, salt, and pepper to make the meatball mixture. Divide the mixture evenly so the balls are of equal size.

4 Place the raw meatballs in the simmering sauce and cook for 2 to 3 hours. During the cooking time, some fat may rise to the surface and will need to be carefully skimmed.

5 Taste the gravy and season as necessary. Remove the meat and serve on the side in a serving dish.

Manicotti with Marinara Sauce
✑ *Dina Altieri* ✑
NEW ENGLAND CULINARY INSTITUTE, ESSEX JUNCTION, VERMONT

This recipe is about as close to any chef's heart as a recipe can be. Dina Altieri (pictured with her grandmother, left), now a chef/instructor at the New England Culinary Institute in Vermont, grew up surrounded by exuberant Italian cooks, most notably her grandmother. While the men and boys played sports and spent time outside, the women gathered in the kitchen around the big family table near the stove to cook and gossip. Dina loved the warm and comforting feelings of being in the kitchen with her mother, grandmother, and aunts while they talked their way through dish after dish, guided less by recipes than by memories of holiday meals gone by.

This manicotti recipe belonged to Dina's grandmother, who passed away recently. When Dina's family was going through her grandparents' belongings at their home in New Jersey, Dina's mom came across an old box of recipes. The manicotti recipe card was the only one Dina took home with her that day in spite of the fact that her mother offered her the entire box. It is one of her most prized possessions.

SERVES 10

SAUCE
1 medium onion, diced small
2 tablespoons extra virgin olive oil
4 cloves garlic, minced
2 tablespoons dried basil
2 tablespoons dried parsley
1 tablespoon dried oregano
1 (28-ounce) can crushed tomatoes
1 (15-ounce) can tomato sauce

1 (12-ounce) can tomato paste
Salt and black pepper to taste

CRÊPES
1 cup all-purpose flour
1 teaspoon salt
4 eggs

FILLING
½ pound mozzarella, freshly grated
4 tablespoons freshly grated Parmesan
1½ pounds whole-milk ricotta cheese

1 or 2 eggs
3 tablespoons finely chopped fresh
   Italian parsley
Salt and black pepper to taste

1 For the marinara sauce, sweat the onion in olive oil over medium heat in a large saucepan until translucent. Add the garlic, spices, all of the tomato products, and 2 cups of water. Season to taste with salt and pepper and simmer for 2 to 3 hours.

2 For the crêpe batter, combine the flour and salt in a mixing bowl and make a well in the center. Add 1 cup of water and the eggs to the center well and whisk gently just until the ingredients are incorporated. Let rest for 30 minutes in the refrigerator.

3 Meanwhile, prepare the filling by combining the mozzarella, Parmesan, and ricotta cheeses with the eggs, parsley, salt, and pepper. Set aside.

4 To prepare the crêpes, use an 8-inch Teflon-coated sauté pan greased with a small amount of vegetable oil. Gently heat the pan and ladle a scant ¼ cup of batter into the pan, swirling immediately to disperse the batter evenly. Cook gently without browning on both sides. Let the crêpe cool slightly on a plate while cooking the next one. Stack the crêpes one on top of the other until all the batter is used (approximately 20 crêpes). The crêpes may be made in advance, and if wrapped tightly, can be refrigerated for up to one week and frozen for up to one month.

5 Preheat the oven to 350° F.

6 Fill each crêpe with approximately two tablespoons of filling and roll into a tube shape.

7 Cover the bottom of a large baking dish with a thin layer of marinara. Place the manicotti in rows on top of the marinara and cover each one with additional sauce. Bake for 30 to 40 minutes, or until the sauce is bubbling.

8 Serve the manicotti with remaining marinara sauce and additional grated Parmesan cheese sprinkled on top.

Chicken Cutlets
~ Dina Altieri ~
NEW ENGLAND CULINARY INSTITUTE, ESSEX JUNCTION, VERMONT

When Dina Altieri and her spouse, Sara, first got together, Dina felt strongly that they needed to create a family atmosphere in the kitchen, so the two of them cook together every night. Finding a home with a separate dining room was a top priority during their house hunt when they moved to Vermont, and they've gone to great lengths to make their dining room beautiful and welcoming. Dina loves the warm yellow color Sara picked, and it is one of the most used rooms in the house. While they eat a wide variety of foods, one of Dina's favorite meals is still Chicken Cutlets with mashed potatoes like her mother used to make.

⊰ KITCHEN MEMORIES ⊱

When I was growing up, my mother (pictured above) took the family meals very seriously. I think I was twelve before she finally went to work, so she was there during my formative years, and the evening meal was a big deal. There were at least two courses every night. I was very unlike any of my childhood friends. That was the age of microwaves. At our house Ma would make veal chops or cook steak for dinner or make a pasta main course. She put a lot of effort into the meal. There was always a main protein, a starch, and a vegetable. Typically it was a salad course or a pasta course, and the main course was meat. I look back on it now and I think, "Oh, my God, I don't have the patience for that after a long day! Even after she went to work, she still managed to put together a meal like that."

4 (4-ounce) skinless and boneless
   chicken breasts
Salt and pepper to taste
¼ cup all-purpose flour

2 eggs, slightly beaten
¼ cup bread crumbs
½ cup vegetable oil

1 Rinse the chicken breasts and pat dry.

2 Using a mallet, pound the chicken breasts until they are ¼ inch thick.

3 Season both sides with salt and pepper.

4 Place the flour, eggs, and bread crumbs into three separate mixing bowls.

5 Coat each chicken breast with flour. Shake off any excess flour and place the chicken breast in the bowl with the beaten eggs. Coat the chicken breast evenly on both sides with egg, then place into the bowl with the bread crumbs. Lightly coat the chicken breast with bread crumbs and place on a clean plate. Repeat the breading procedure for each chicken breast.

6 Heat oil over medium heat in a 10-inch sauté pan until the oil begins to "gently move" (approximately 325° F).

7 Pan-fry each of the chicken breasts, two at a time, in the pan. Don't overcrowd the pan or the oil will cool down and the cutlets will become saturated with fat. The cutlets will cook halfway on one side and will need to be flipped for even cooking on the other side. The approximate cooking time is 3 minutes per side.

8 Once the chicken cutlets have reached an internal temperature of 160° F, remove them from the oil and place them on a plate lined with paper towels. Serve. Dina loves these cutlets with ketchup or freshly squeezed lemon.

Mom's Secret Dina makes the cutlets for Sara, who is wheat- and lactose-intolerant, without the use of wheat-flour-based bread crumbs simply by substituting bread crumbs from their homemade rice bread.

Potato Rolls

Lucia Watson

LUCIA'S RESTAURANT AND WINE BAR, MINNEAPOLIS

Lucia Watson's grandmother was an incredible baker, and Lucia has found inspiration for her own cooking in the summers she and her family spent at their cabin at Lake Raney in northern Minnesota. These Potato Rolls are a dressed-up version of the kind her grandmother used to make there.

MAKES ABOUT 30 ROLLS

2 small russet potatoes, peeled and
  cut into chunks
2 packages active dry yeast
2 tablespoons plus a pinch sugar
1 cup buttermilk, at room temperature

6 tablespoons (¾ stick) unsalted butter,
  melted and cooled, plus extra to
  grease the bowl
4 teaspoons salt
5½ to 6½ cups bread flour, plus more
  for the work surface

1 Cook the potatoes in simmering water until fork tender. Drain and reserve ½ cup of the liquid. Mash the potatoes and set aside.

2 Cool the reserved liquid to lukewarm temperature. Place the liquid, yeast, and a pinch of sugar in bowl. Let sit until foamy.

3 Add the remaining sugar, buttermilk, 4 tablespoons of the butter, and the salt. Gradually add enough flour to make a sticky dough. Knead until smooth. Brush a mixing bowl with butter and place the dough in, turning to coat. Let it rise until double, about 1 to 1½ hours.

4 Preheat the oven to 375° F. Line three baking sheets with parchment paper. Roll out the dough to ¾ inch thick. Cut the dough into 2-inch-wide strips. Cut strips into a total of 30 triangles or squares and place on the prepared baking sheets.

5 Brush the tops with the remaining butter and cover with plastic wrap. Let rise for about 15 minutes. Remove plastic wrap. Bake until golden, about 15 minutes. Serve hot.

GARLIC AND ROSEMARY KNOT VARIATION

¾ cup extra virgin olive oil   2 cloves garlic, minced
3 tablespoons fresh rosemary, chopped   ½ teaspoon fresh black pepper

1 Combine all of the ingredients.

2 After cutting the potato dough into wide strips, dip each strip of dough into
the oil mixture then tie into a knot. Bake according to the directions above.

⊰ KITCHEN MEMORIES ⊱

I think that the strongest influence on my sensibility as a chef today—which
comes directly from my grandmother and my family experiences at Lake
Raney—is an appreciation for, and a real objectivity about, ingredients. I think
a lot of times as chefs we see too much food. It comes in cases and cases and you
see whole cows and giant hams and you lose your objective, discerning eye
about what's really good and what's not. I try to be vigilant and pound it into my
chefs that you need to keep an objective eye for your food. You need to not mar its
essential quality with fancy stuff. Stacking food or confusing flavors is unnatu-
ral—first of all you're not respecting the food and second, I think most diners
don't really get it. They would rather have something they understand and something that affects them in an honest palate way. They should be able to taste it
and say, "Wow, this is really good!" Even if it's something common like beef tenderloin with béarnaise sauce, you want them to say it's the best béarnaise sauce
they've ever had, because it's made with really great butter from a few miles
away and great tarragon from a nearby farm or kitchen garden. If you don't
have good butter and tarragon, you might as well just make something else. I
really think that has to do with seeing my grandmother's frugality and the
appreciation I learned for food through doing things out at the lake, like having
to pick blueberries because it's too far to go to town. Every blueberry is really
precious. And there's an excitement about it. You get to pick them and go back
and form them into muffins and then eat the muffins and think, "God, I picked
these and they're really magical and delicious." It's fun. I think all that goes
right into my philosophy today.

Smoked Salmon-Cardamom Spread

Kirsten and Mandy Dixon

WINTERLAKE LODGE, REDOUBT BAY LODGE, AND RIVERSONG LODGE, ALASKA

Kirsten grew up in the "corridor of convenience foods" in America's culinary history, so her mother didn't do a lot of cooking at home. With her father in the military and later a member of the State Department, however, Kirsten had ample opportunity to develop her palate as she traveled around the world with her family. At an early age she was unusually intrigued by food and flavor—so much so that in her middle teens, she began cooking from Julia Child's *A to Z* as her Friday-night activity. Her friends loved the final product but were bored with the process and would often protest, begging to go see a movie instead.

After college, Kirsten moved to Alaska, where, with her husband Carl, she was to set out on a great adventure in the wilderness. The couple bought Riversong Lodge, located miles from any city. Kirsten was only twenty-four years old and knew nothing about the hospitality industry, but she was excited and motivated to try something new.

Since there was no one in her community to teach her about cooking, Kirsten did most of her initial learning through books and magazines. Over the years her cooking has evolved from basic-buffet style country ham and mashed potatoes to something uniquely regional and personal, and she has passed her culinary knowledge on to her daughter, Mandy, who recently attended culinary school and works in the family's three restaurants.

The older of the two siblings, Carly works as the front house manager of Riversong Lodge. She takes her job very seriously, interacting with guests and doing her best to make them feel comfortable throughout their stay. She is also responsible for hiring, and management of staff, and she's only twenty-one years old.

The recipe that follows is an excellent example of the type of fare Mandy and Kirsten create in their lodge kitchens. They love cardamom and use it often with salmon. Kirsten says that the combination of sour cream, lemon, and cardamom is very complementary to the strong flavor of salmon.

MAKES 1 1/2 POUNDS

1 pound kippered (hot-smoked) salmon
¾ cup sour cream
½ teaspoon ground cardamom
Freshly ground pepper to taste
1 lemon

1 Chop one-half of the kippered salmon in the bowl of a food processor. Add the sour cream, cardamom, and pepper. Grate the zest of the lemon into the salmon mixture. Squeeze half of the lemon's juices into the mixture as well. Process the salmon mixture until it is pureed. Transfer the puree to a large bowl.

2 Coarsely chop the remaining salmon and add it to the puree. Mix well, cover, and refrigerate until serving time. Serve a dollop of the spread on your favorite crackers or bread.

⊰ KITCHEN MEMORIES ⊱

As a child I lived with my family in Europe and southeast Asia, and I think it was that more than anything that led me to be interested in food. When we came back from living in southeast Asia, we lived in the Bay Area in San Francisco, and on weekends my father and I would often go and hunt out small Thai or Vietnamese restaurants, which were not as ubiquitous in the mid-1970s. We were looking for opportunities to have true ethnic cuisine from places we had been. We still take great pleasure in hunting down that Korean hole-in-the-wall with the lady cooking on a portable burner in the back room. My father works for me in the summer in Alaska. He's seventy-six years old, and he still flies up from upstate New York every summer and loads and unloads our airplanes and shops for us. He's also our expeditor.

Orange and Apple Noodle Kugel
⟳ *Alison Awerbuch* ⟳

ABIGAIL KIRSCH CULINARY PRODUCTIONS, TARRYTOWN, NEW YORK

For Alison Awerbuch, food and cooking were integral to family life. Her Polish, Russian, and Jewish heritage is rich with culinary tradition, and all the women on both sides of her family were great cooks, although the most influential was her mother. Throughout Alison's childhood her mother was known amongst her friends as a true gourmet cook, and she reveled in all aspects of entertaining, from menu planning to table setting—all the way down to labeling platters in advance of a dinner party so she'd know exactly what would go where when it came time to serve the meal. Alison spent a lot of time in the kitchen at her mother's side when she was a little girl and recalls visiting the Eastern Farmers' Market in Detroit, where her mother would look for the freshest, most interesting produce and dairy products. She marveled at how comfortable her mother was deviating from a printed recipe and spent a lot of her free time helping out in the kitchen. As a teenager she traveled with her mother to Europe, where they spent a month exploring not only the museums, churches, and back roads of France and Italy but also the open-air food markets and specialty food shops, which her mom researched in advance and where they bought and sampled foods indigenous to the area. They even spent time cooking in some private Tuscan kitchens.

Shortly after their trip to Europe, Alison decided that what she really wanted to do was cook, and she somehow knew that she preferred catering to restaurant work. After a couple of years in college, she settled on her career and today works for one of New York's most successful catering companies, Abigail Kirsch Culinary Productions.

Alison's mother gave her a book when she left home to attend the Culinary Institute of America in 1981. It was a compilation of family recipes, and has become a treasured family heirloom that Alison plans to pass down to the next generation. This is one of the recipes included in the book, dedicated simply, "To my darling daughter, Alison. With Love. 1981." The recipe makes enough for a large family to share.

ORANGE AND APPLE NOODLE KUGEL
1# Wide Noodles Cooked, Not rinsed
2 C Orange Juice (Use a little Concentrated)
1 C Sugar   2 Tsp. Cinnamon
6 T Melted Butter   4 Beaten Eggs
2 Grated Apples   1 Tsp. Salt
1/2 C Raisins (Opt)

Topping:
1/2 Tsp. Cinnamon   1/2 C Brown Sugar
                     1/4 C Walnuts, Chopped

Cook noodles. Melt butter and toss with noodles and combine with orange juice, sugar and cinnamon mixture while noodles are hot.
Set aside and marinate for 1 hour stirring occas.
Add Eggs, Apples and Salt.
Pour into buttered casserole.
Sprinkle on topping.
Bake uncovered 350o - 1 hour.

SERVES 8 TO 12

1 pound wide noodles

6 tablespoons (¾ stick) unsalted butter, melted

2 cups orange juice

1 cup granulated sugar

2 teaspoons ground cinnamon

½ cup raisins (optional)

4 eggs, beaten

2 apples, grated

1 teaspoon salt

TOPPING

½ teaspoon ground cinnamon

½ cup light or dark brown sugar

¼ cup chopped walnuts

1 In a large pot of boiling water, cook the noodles. While the noodles are cooking, melt the butter. Drain the noodles, but do not rinse. Transfer to a large bowl and toss with butter.

2 While the noodles are still hot, combine the orange juice, sugar, and cinnamon and add to the noodles. Set aside and allow to marinate for 1 hour, stirring occasionally.

3 Preheat the oven to 350° F and butter a 9 x 12-inch casserole dish. Add the raisins (if using), eggs, apples, and salt to the marinated noodle mixture and pour into the buttered casserole.

4 In a small bowl, combine the cinnamon, brown sugar, and walnuts. Sprinkle the mixture on top of the noodles and bake, uncovered, for 1 hour.

Linguine alle Vongole

LINGUINI WITH CLAM SAUCE

Lidia Bastianich

FELIDIA & BECCO, NEW YORK
LIDIA'S ITALY, PITTSBURGH & KANSAS CITY, MISSOURI

Lidia Bastianich is all about family: Her culinary inspiration comes straight from her heritage, her mother (pictured with Lidia, below) still lives with her, her children have both left home and come back to be a part of her business in one way or another, and her grandchildren are growing up in her kitchens the same way her own children did. This recipe is a family favorite.

I have five grandchildren: Olivia is six, Lorenzo is five, Miles is four, Ethan is two, and Julia is one. We cook all the time at my house—every Saturday or Sunday if I'm not traveling. My daughter comes Saturday, too, because she's within walking distance, but my son and all his kids come only on Sunday. We all get into the act. Sometimes I work late so grandma (my mother) and I make plans. She's my sous-chef. She gets things going for me in the morning, makes the stock for me, then I get up and finish it. My daughter and daughter-in-law always help clean up. The grandchildren love it! Sometimes they'll just pull up a chair or they have their aprons on, and I give them chores. When they come in, or sometimes before they get here, we'll talk and I'll ask them what they want to eat. They like to make gnocchi with me, they like chicken and potatoes or linguine with clam sauce, they like a good chicken soup with pastina, and they love spinach and broccoli. Sometimes I just fry potatoes and eggs. They even enjoy vegetable soups. I like to expose them to different things, not just what they know they're going to like.

SERVES 4

3½ pounds fresh clams, cleaned
6 tablespoons olive oil
3 cloves garlic, minced
½ cup dry white wine
Freshly ground pepper to taste

¼ cup fresh Italian parsley, cleaned
  and minced
1 pound linguine
Crushed red pepper to taste

1 Shuck the clams, reserving the liquid. Make sure the meat has no shells, and if desired, mince. Drain the clam juice through cheesecloth or a very fine strainer to remove grit.

2 In a large skillet, heat the oil and sauté the garlic. Add the clam juice, wine, and pepper. Bring to a boil and cook on high heat for 4 minutes. Add the parsley and clams and boil for 2 more minutes.

3 In the meantime, cook the linguine in salted boiling water until al dente (9 to 12 minutes, depending on brand). Drain, toss in the clams, sprinkle with crushed red pepper, and serve.

Hickory House Deviled Eggs
∽ *Deann and Lanie Bayless* ∽
FRONTERA GRILL AND TOPOLOBAMPO, CHICAGO

Twice a year the Bayless family puts together a special barbecue meal for kids from Lanie's class that has its roots in Rick's family's restaurant. Deann loves it because it's a great way to get to know Lanie's friends and their families, and it gives everyone a chance to spend some family time together in a relaxed environment. It's always the same meal and Lanie always takes a major role in the cooking. These deviled eggs are from that menu. Lanie loves them and says that "any kid, any adult, any person will like these. Or if they don't—I certainly wouldn't understand why."

⊰ KITCHEN MEMORIES ⊱

Cooking at home is a huge part of our lives, although we don't do it as often as we like. Sitting down to one meal a day that we have made, simple or complicated, is really important. In our schedule what's worked out most often is breakfast. It's not long, and it may just be a poured bowl of cereal, but we each have one with some fruit or whatever and we sit down together for this connection time. We say grace. There's a formality around it—a symbol of family, of what it means to be around the table. Then on weekends and on special occasions we do more elaborate things. Right from the beginning Lanie's always liked to be in the middle helping. I wouldn't say she's a passionate cook who wants to know every nuance, but she loves being in the middle of the action. Rick bought her her first knife when she was five. We've not dumbed it down for her, but we've tried to do things that are appropriate for her at each level and now she is a decent cook. At thirteen she can hold her own just fine.

I think food can help pull families together. I know this one mom who says that when her son was a teenager she was always cooking, and his friends always wanted to be around because there was always good food around. Sharing meals grounds you in a very specific way. I'm sure it will grate on Lanie eventually as it did me. I didn't appreciate it then, but I did later when I got out of the dorm and into an apartment.

1 medium red potato, peeled and
   cut into 8 pieces
6 eggs
1 tablespoon salt, plus additional salt
   to taste

1 tablespoon yellow mustard
2 tablespoons mayonnaise
2 tablespoons sweet pickle relish
Chopped chives or purple chive
   blossoms for garnish

1 Place the potato and eggs in a medium saucepan. Fill with enough cold water to cover the eggs by 1 inch. Add 1 tablespoon of salt (to keep the eggs from cracking). Set over medium-high heat. When the water comes to a simmer, in about 10 minutes, reduce the heat to medium-low. The water

> *Mom's Secret* Removing a yolk is much easier when it's not all the way on one side. It should be more in the center. Stir the eggs gently while hard-boiling them to keep the yolks in the center.

should stay at a very gentle simmer so the eggs don't come out tough. Cook for 9 minutes. Use a slotted spoon to remove the potato to a medium-size bowl, then set the pan, still containing the eggs, under cold running water for 3 minutes.

2 Add the mustard, mayonnaise, and relish to the potato and mash together with a fork. Peel the cold eggs and cut them in half lengthwise, then use a small fork or spoon to scoop out the yolks carefully, adding them to the mustard mixture. Mash the yolks thoroughly into the mustard mixture. Taste the filling and add more salt if desired.

3 Use a fork to fill the hollow boiled egg whites, mounding the filling slightly, and covering the whole cut side of each egg white. Drag a fork lengthwise down the egg to make pretty ridges. Arrange on a platter and garnish with chopped chives or purple chive blossoms, or decorate with little pansies.

Sicilian-Style Chard with Tomatoes and Garlic
❧ *Elizabeth Germain* ❧

We think the business world drives people into the kitchen, because we've interviewed a large number of chefs who started out in business and finance and ended up cooking for a living. Elizabeth Germain (pictured, left) is one of those people. The first generation in her Italian and English family to go to college, Elizabeth earned her CPA and headed off to work for Arthur Anderson, where she remained for five years, until she realized she just wasn't passionate about crunching numbers. A different sort of crunching seemed more apropos to a woman who still cherished the first Girl Scout badge she ever earned—in cooking, of course!

Elizabeth started out in the restaurant business at the front of the house, applying her business skills on a practical level, but in the late 1980s her career took another surprising turn after she was struck with Epstein-Barr Syndrome. For health reasons Elizabeth made some major changes to her diet and reconnected with the food of her heritage. She saw undeniable common sense in the ways in which her grandparents handled their food. She was impressed both by the "lifeforce and vitality" of the foods her family ate as well as the "spiritual dimension" in which it was honored and shared. Elizabeth's new focus in her writing and her work as a professional chef is on promoting an awareness of local, seasonal, and sustainable farming and eating.

Elizabeth tells us this chard recipe is a longtime family favorite. Her Sicilian grandmother stewed the chard and tomatoes that were grown in their backyard by her Sicilian grandfather. She likens it to a lighter version of southern-style collard greens and says that "long, slow simmering in a large amount of liquid yields chard that is very tender, sweet, and earthy tasting." Not all the cooking liquid is used in the finished dish, and Elizabeth's grandparents taught her to drink the excess, a "delicious and nutritious elixir." Even if you're not making it for your whole family, go ahead and cook the whole recipe—the leftovers are fantastic!

2 pounds chard, washed and shaken to remove excess water, stems separated from leaves

1½ teaspoons salt, plus additional salt to taste

3 tablespoons olive oil

6 large garlic cloves, sliced thin (about 3 tablespoons)

6 medium ripe tomatoes (about 3 pounds), blanched, peeled, most seeds removed, and diced large (about 3 cups); or 1 (28-ounce) can diced tomatoes

1 teaspoon crushed red pepper flakes (optional)

1 Trim and cut the chard stems into 3-inch-long pieces. Stack and roll the chard leaves, and cut them into 3-inch-wide pieces. Set aside.

2 Bring 1½ quarts of water to a boil over high heat in a Dutch oven or other deep pot. Add the salt and chard stems, and stir with a wooden spoon to immerse the stems in water. Bring to a simmer, reduce the heat to medium, cover, and simmer for 5 to 10 minutes, depending on the thickness of the stems. Add the leaves in batches, gently stirring with a wooden spoon to help them wilt into the water. When all the leaves are wilted, bring back to a simmer, cover, and cook for 10 minutes. Place a colander over a large bowl. Pour the chard and its cooking liquid into the colander, reserving the liquid in the bowl. Set both aside.

3 Return the pot to the stove and heat the oil over medium heat. Add the garlic and cook until fragrant and lightly browned, stirring occasionally, about 4 minutes. Stir in the tomatoes (and optional red pepper flakes); season to taste with salt. Add the chard, stir to mix with the tomatoes and garlic, cover, and simmer for 5 minutes. Add 2 to 3 cups of the reserved liquid (depending on how soupy you wish the dish to be), cover, and simmer until the greens are very tender, about 10 minutes. Season to taste with salt (and optional red pepper flakes) and serve in soup bowls. Refrigerate leftovers; reheat in a covered pot over medium heat until hot.

Mom's Secret To remove the chard stems, hold each leaf by the stem with the leaf pointing down. Use a knife to slash on either side of the stem to cut away the green leafy portion. Older chard has larger and fleshier stems, which take longer to cook. Use chard with white, red, or rainbow-colored stems.

Gram's Stuffed Breast of Veal
≈ *Gloria Ciccarone-Nehls* ≈
HUNTINGTON HOTEL, SAN FRANCISCO

Gloria Ciccarone-Nehls was born into the restaurant business. In the 1930s her grandmother started cooking traditional Italian dishes like spaghetti and meatballs for servicemen in her home over a filling station in Bethel, Connecticut. Over time the men began making requests for various dishes, and she became known around town for her cooking. Someone suggested that she look into buying the property next to hers, the Avalon Inn, to open a restaurant, and she did. There were cabins for rent and she always had a live band, making it one of the area's hot spots. In the 1940s she sold it to Gloria's father, who transformed it into a finer dining establishment featuring Continental cuisine. The restaurant remained in the family for forty-two years.

Gloria grew up there and began working in the restaurant when she was just eleven years old. By the time she was thirteen she was running the pantry station. With 350 seats it was a huge responsibility for such a young girl, but she liked it well enough to go back and work for her father after she completed art school. In 1976 she left again to attend the Culinary Institute of America. She graduated early, moved to San Francisco, and has been there ever since, at the Huntington Hotel.

This veal dish was always served to large crowds at family gatherings and was almost always served chilled and sliced. Gloria says there were never enough bones to go around, so she would always consider herself very lucky to have one included on her plate.

SERVES 20

2 cups golden raisins
½ cup white wine
1 breast of veal, approximately
    12 pounds, bone in, pocketed by
    the butcher for stuffing
Salt to taste
1 tablespoon white pepper
    (plus more to taste)
Zest of 2 lemons

3 tablespoons chopped garlic
2 cups diced yellow onions
½ cup olive oil
1½ cups chopped fresh Italian parsley
¼ cup chopped fresh basil
1 gallon stale, cubed white or wheat bread
2 cups pine nuts, lightly toasted
12 eggs
1 cup grated Parmesan cheese

1 Soak the raisins in white wine for about an hour.

2 Rub the inside and outside of the veal with a little salt, the white pepper, lemon zest, and 2 table-spoons of the garlic (reserving the third tablespoon for the stuffing).

3 Sauté the onion in the olive oil over medium-high heat in a large saucepan until soft. Add the pars-ley, basil, and remaining tablespoon of garlic. Season with salt and pep-per. Sauté briefly and pour over the bread. Mix well and add the soaked raisins and pine nuts. Add the eggs and mix until the stuffing is soft. Add the cheese and mix again.

4 Preheat the oven to 400° F. Stuff the mixture evenly into the cavity of the veal, taking care not to overstuff the breast. Secure the opening with bamboo skewers. Rub the outside of the breast with olive oil. Place in an oiled roasting pan with ¼ inch of water in the bottom and roast for 30 minutes before reducing the heat to 375° F. Cook for another 90 minutes. The juices should run clear when the meat is pierced with a knife.

5 Chill the roast overnight in the refrigerator or enjoy it after it has been allowed to rest at room temperature for 15 minutes.

6 To serve: Slice the veal horizontally along the bone until the breast is sepa-rated from the bone. Slice the breast into ¾-inch slices. Cut through the rib bones and lay them on a serving platter. Arrange the sliced veal on top of the bones. Serve with Roasted Garlic Aïoli (recipe follows).

Mom's Secret Because every piece of veal will vary, you may or may not need all of the stuffing. It is, however, best not to try and fit it all in if you think it's too much. The whole breast, on the bone, after being stuffed, should be about 4½ to 5½ inches thick.

AÏOLI

MAKES 2 CUPS

1½ cups olive oil, plus additional oil
    as needed

¼ cup garlic cloves, peeled

3 egg yolks (pasteurized egg yolks must
    be used because the aïoli is not
    cooked)

½ teaspoon chopped garlic

1½ teaspoons white vinegar

1½ teaspoons fresh lemon juice

½ teaspoon salt

pinch white pepper

½ teaspoon dry mustard

1 In a small saucepan, combine the olive oil and garlic cloves. Cook over medium-low heat on the stovetop until the cloves are soft but not browned. Remove the cloves and allow them to cool. Strain the oil and refrigerate it until cold. You should have about 1¼ cups. If not, add more olive oil.

2 Begin processing the egg yolks, chopped garlic, and reserved poached garlic cloves in a food processor. While it is running add about a teaspoon of vinegar. After that is well mixed, add a few tablespoons of the garlic oil to stabilize the emulsification. Alternating a few drops at a time, add the remaining vinegar and oil into the aïoli until it thickens. Then, with processor running, add remaining oil in a slow steady stream. If the aïoli is too thick, you can thin it out with a tablespoon of hot water. Add lemon juice, salt, pepper, and mustard and process briefly just to combine. Remove from the food processor and chill. This sauce should be served cold alongside Gram's Stuffed Breast of Veal (page 90).

⊰ KITCHEN MEMORIES ⊱

When I was at the CIA, I would always bring other kids home to work at the restaurant. I went back every weekend to make money. My mother (pictured on the previous page) was so funny; being a nurse by trade, she'd call them all into the banquet room and tell them all, "You know, you shouldn't become a chef, it's too hard on your body," and to the girls especially, "You'll get varicose veins!" and they'd come out looking like they were going to cry. I'd say, "Mom, what are you saying to my friends?" and she'd say, "Oh, nothing." She also used to sew us up when we cut our fingers. It was busy, we couldn't leave. We'd go back in the office, she'd stitch us up, put a glove on us, and we'd go back to work.

Râpé Pie
Maureen Pothier
JOHNSON & WALES, PROVIDENCE, RHODE ISLAND

There were nine kids in Maureen Pothier's family, and her mother did lots of cooking every day, starting with a breakfast of eggs, oatmeal, or cream of wheat. Once the kids were out the door to school, she barely had time to straighten up the mess from breakfast before she was making lunch for the troops who walked the mile home from St. Margaret's school at noontime every day. At the end of the day the kids would march (or more likely meander) home again for cookies or another snack before Maureen's mom started cooking dinner, which was done in two shifts—one for the kids and one for Maureen's father. She literally cooked all day, which Maureen believes sparked her own interest in food. On Sundays her father cooked johnnycakes and eggs, and all the kids helped out.

In spite of her early interest in cooking, Maureen entered the professional world by happenstance. At a crossroads in her life, in the midst of a divorce and working at a children's library, she was trying to decide whether she would go back to do something for her own personal growth. Remembering how much she enjoyed cooking and being in her mother's kitchen, she decided to apply to the Rhode Island School of Design's culinary program, not to start a career but to take a break from life. During her first year there she realized she needed to take a job to help pay her bills and found one at Bluepoint Oyster Bar, which caused a shift in her career thinking.

A trip to Italy to visit wine bars with some colleagues who were thinking of opening one next door to Bluepoint led her to seek out Madeleine Kamman, who invited her to apply to her short, but intense, cooking program. Maureen was accepted. Maureen attended the four-and-a-half month class and returned to her job at Bluepoint Oyster Bar. Later Maureen received a Beringer Scholarship which enabled her to attend another of Madeleine's classes, and received her associate's degree from Johnson & Wales. Today she is a culinary instructor there.

Râpé Pie is the ultimate family recipe because it requires the coordinated efforts of many pairs of hands. It is a traditional favorite of Maureen's family, served on New Year's Day.

20 pounds whole chickens (a lot of
    small fryers, rather than a couple of
    large roasters, make a better stock)
3 medium-size carrots
3 large celery ribs
3 large Spanish onions
2 bay leaves
Salt and pepper to taste
40 pounds Prince Edward Island
    potatoes (do not substitute
    another variety)

3 pounds lean salt pork, frozen
1½ pounds boneless pork loin slices

SPECIAL EQUIPMENT NEEDED:
3 or 4 hand-held potato graters
    (these are specialized graters made
    of wire mesh that can be purchased
    at kitchen specialty stores and various
    online retail outlets)
15 x 10 x 5-inch roasting pan
Cheesecloth

1 Make a chicken stock: Place the chickens, carrots, celery, onions, and bay leaves in a stockpot (you may need 2 pots). Cover the ingredients with water and bring to a boil, then lower the heat to a simmer. Continually skim off any scum that rises to the top. Cook gently for 4 to 5 hours, until the stock is very flavorful and the chicken is still moist. Strain the stock, skim the fat, then season heavily with salt and pepper. When you taste the stock it should taste too salty. (This is very important; otherwise the finished pie will be bland.) Pick the chicken off of the bones in large pieces, discarding skin and bones; set meat aside.

2 With 3 or 4 people and as many hand-held graters, peel the potatoes. Set each grater in a deep bowl or container and grate (râpé) the potatoes in a circular motion. Do not go up and down or you will get strips of potato instead of a smooth grate, which will compromise the texture.

3 As soon as the potatoes are grated, put about 4 cups at a time into a large double square of cheesecloth and gently squeeze to remove (and discard) most of the juice. Try not to get it too dry.

4 Put the potato "pulp" in a large bowl and gently mix in enough boiling chicken stock to remoisten (the stock must be hot when it is added to the potatoes). It's important to remoisten with chicken stock immediately to keep the potatoes from turning brown. To determine when it's moist enough, make an indentation about an inch deep into the potatoes with a spoon; when the liquid pools about

Mom's Secret A food processor can be substituted for the graters for similar results using the blade (do not use the grater attachment), however the texture will not be traditional.

halfway in the hole, it's just right. Continue steps 2, 3, and 4 until all of the potatoes are used. (That's where all of the helpers come in!)

5 Meanwhile, remove the rind from 2 pounds of the salt pork, cut it into ¼-inch slices (easier to slice if frozen), and place the slices on the bottom and sides of the roasting pan at 1-inch intervals. In a large skillet on the stovetop, brown the pork loin slices well on both sides, then cut them into bite-size pieces; set aside.

6 To assemble the pie: Preheat the oven to 350° F. Place a layer of potatoes about 1½ inches deep in the bottom of the pan, top with a good layer of chicken, then another layer of potatoes, and so on, until all potatoes are used up and the pan is full. Put the browned pork loin in the middle layer with the chicken. Top the pie with a few more slices of salt pork and bake the pie for 4 hours, or until well browned and bubbly on the top.

7 Dice the remaining salt pork into small (⅓-inch) cubes and brown to cracklings in a sauté pan. Cut the hot pie into squares and serve with butter and hot cracklings in their fat on the side.

⊰ KITCHEN MEMORIES ⊱

My father was Nova Scotian, and we have this Nova Scotian dish every New Year's Day. It's mainly potatoes, grated, but there's a certain way you grate them—you can't just go up and down, you have to go in circles, and there's a special grater for it. Everything goes into a great big pan, probably 2 feet by 3 feet and about 10 inches deep. My sister still has it to this day because she's taken over the Râpé Pie making for the family these days. We always did all the gizzards—we are big gizzard fans in the family—so we'd hide them in special parts of the pie so we'd know where they were when we got our piece. It gets this weird green color but it's so delicious! Then you take it and put a nice big pat of butter on the top and on top of the butter you put salt pork cracklings (had to keep warm up there in Nova Scotia)! The tradition started with my grandmother and then my mother did it and now my sister does it. We all get together and have Râpé Pie every New Year's. The nieces and nephews used to taste it and say, "Ewwww, I don't want to eat this!" The great thing now is that they have been coming at eight in the morning and helping with the râpéing so that when my sister and I get too old, they'll be able to take over the tradition.

Butter Roast Chicken with Fresh Herbs
❧ *Anne Willan* ❧

Anne Willan's mother hated cooking, so the family, as Anne puts it, "had a fat old cook who spent her whole life in the kitchen." She remembers it as a lovely warm place with dishes to lick and describes herself as a "tiny child who was desperately greedy," noting that she's always loved to eat. Cooking was not part of the general education in England where Anne grew up, but between preliminary school and university, Anne attended a finishing school that was affiliated with the Cordon Bleu. She later immigrated to the United States with just $500 in her pocket and in 1964 paid her bills teaching private cooking classes. She also began working for *Gourmet* magazine at that time. Her children, Simon and Emma, were born in 1970 and 1972. In 1975 Anne and her family moved to France and opened the renowned cooking school, La Varenne, which is still in operation today.

Although cooking wasn't a family affair when Anne was a young girl, she began cooking with her own children when they were very young. Today Anne is often separated from her now-adult children, but every time they all get together, the first thing they eat is roast chicken. It's a Willan family comfort food.

SERVES 4 TO 6

1 roasting chicken, about 4 to 5 pounds
1 bunch of fresh herbs, plus some for
   decoration (optional)

Salt and pepper for seasoning
¼ cup (½ stick) unsalted butter, softened
3 cups chicken stock

1 Preheat the oven to 425° F.

2 Wipe the inside of the chicken with paper towels. Fold back the neck skin and use the point of a small knife to scrape free and remove the wishbone. This will make the breast meat easier to carve in neat slices. If you are using soft herb leaves such as sage, tarragon, or parsley, slide your fingers under the breast skin, loosening it from the meat without tearing it, and insert a few herb leaves in a pretty pattern.

3 Season the bird inside and out with salt and pepper, and put a bunch of herbs in the cavity. Truss the bird with a trussing needle, or by simply tying it with string so it holds a neat shape.

4 Set the bird on its back in a medium roasting pan (not too large or the juices will scorch). Spread the breast and legs with the softened butter. If you have the giblets, add the neck, gizzard, and heart to the pan to flavor the gravy (reserve the liver for another use). Roast the chicken until it sizzles and starts to brown, 12 to 15 minutes. Turn it onto its breast, baste well with the pan drippings, and return it to the oven. (Roasting breast downwards keeps the meat moist.) Lower the heat to 375° F and continue roasting, basting at least every 10 minutes.

5 After about 30 more minutes, turn the bird onto its back again so the breast skin becomes crispy. Continue roasting for 15 to 30 minutes longer, basting often, until the leg joint feels pliable when you pull the drumstick and the leg meat starts to shrink from the end of the bone. Pierce the chicken with a two-pronged fork, lift it, and tip the juices from the center cavity into the roasting pan. If they run clear, not pink, the bird is done. If pink, continue cooking until they do run clear. Transfer the chicken to a serving dish or carving board, cover it loosely with foil, and keep it warm.

6 For the gravy: Discard all but a tablespoon or two of fat from the pan (some is needed to emulsify and enrich the sauce). Set the roasting pan on a burner, add the stock, and bring to a boil, scraping to dissolve the pan juices. Boil the gravy rapidly for 10 to 15 minutes, until it thickens slightly and the bubbles break more slowly, showing that it is emulsified and concentrated. If it seems thin, continue boiling until it is reduced and well flavored. Strain the gravy into a saucepan, taste, and adjust the seasonings.

7 If you are carving the chicken at the table, discard the cooked herbs from the cavity. If carving in the kitchen, arrange the chicken pieces on a serving dish, moisten them with a little gravy, and pass the rest separately.

Chapter Four
Motherlands

THIS CHAPTER SHOWCASES THE ETHNIC DIVERSITY of the women included in this book. The various regions of the United States as well as the native countries of the women chefs are the inspiration for the dishes found in this chapter and include the flavors of Thailand, China, Mexico, Germany, Hungary, Czechoslovakia, Austria, Morocco, Russia, and England.

Zarela Martinez shared Sopa Seca, her childhood comfort food; Nora Pouillon's Mother's Hearty Hungarian Goulash is a flavorful and filling wintertime dish; Lisa Schroeder's Mireille's Moroccan Salads are a simple, clean, and flavorful way to start a meal, and Olivia Wu's Pork Coated with Anise-Scented Roasted Rice over Sweet Potatoes is authentic and truly delicious.

Travel the world with some of America's greatest chefs without ever having to leave the warmth and comfort of your own kitchen!

Calabacitas Con Queso

(Zucchini with Cheese)

Zarela Martinez

ZARELA RESTAURANT, NEW YORK

Hal Rubenstein of *New York* magazine once described Zarela Martinez as "the true goddess of Mexican cuisine," and New York City diners seem to agree. Zarela grew up on a cattle ranch in Mexico as a tomboy who could kill a rattlesnake with a whip, break broncos, and neuter cattle. She and her mother drove tractors and rode horses, but they also had a tremendous interest in food and meal preparation. Though her heritage is Mexican, Zarela's family also included a Lebanese uncle by marriage, which opened her mother's eyes to a whole new world of cooking. There was also a Chinese restaurant at the U.S.–Mexican border that sparked her interest in Asian cooking. Way back in 1956, she kept a pantry that would intrigue any chef today. It was filled with everything from escargots to water chestnuts and a wide variety of pastas. Her interests were further piqued by Helen Corbett's books and *Gourmet* magazine. Her mother also had a penchant for lovely table settings, and every night the family, which was of modest means, ate off blue Delft china and drank from crystal glasses. Their home was isolated—a five-hour journey to anywhere—and yet they dined on curries, rabbit provençal, and Chinese chicken. There is no question in Zarela's mind about where her passion for food blossomed.

By the age of eight or nine, Zarela was making tortillas, and later, as a college student, Zarela still lived on the ranch alone and threw herself into making jams, molasses, corned beef, and ham. She even learned to make beer before heading off to El Paso to pursue a career in social work. Not long afterward she married a widower with three children and found herself pregnant with twins. To make extra money for her family, she started baking cookies and making dinners for friends. Her mother offered to give Zarela her inheritance early so that she could go to culinary school and make a career for herself. An initial week-long course in Los Angeles gave Zarela a strong foundation in catering, and later a course in New Orleans led to an introduction to Paul Prudhomme. This, in turn, led Zarela to help Prudhomme out at an event at Tavern on the Green, where her rise to stardom officially began. She drew the attention of restaurant mogul Warner LeRoy and *New York Times* writer Craig Claiborne, who helped her develop a menu for a meal she cooked for Queen Elizabeth at the

Ronald Reagan ranch. She moved to New York City with her children in 1983 and took a consulting job, which in 1987 led her to open the restaurant she still owns today.

One of her primary goals in cooking is to preserve the traditions of her homeland, and the following recipes are wonderful examples of Zarela's Mexican heritage. Zarela says that she and her family ate this dish at least once a week, sometimes more, during harvest time, and she would groan when she saw it, but now she loves it because it tastes great and reminds her of home.

SERVES 4 TO 6

1½ pounds zucchini (5 to 6 young, tender zucchini), scrubbed but not peeled
Salt and freshly ground black pepper to taste
2 tablespoons vegetable oil
1 large garlic clove, minced
1 medium onion, finely chopped (about 1 cup)
1 large tomato or 2 small ones (about ¾ pound), chopped

2 cups fresh corn kernels cut from the cob (or one 10-ounce package frozen corn or one 16-ounce can plain corn kernels, drained)
2 poblano chiles, roasted, peeled, and finely chopped
1 (5-ounce can) evaporated milk or ⅓ cup heavy cream
½ pound white Cheddar cheese, finely diced

1 Cut the zucchini into small (about ¼-inch) dice. Place in a medium saucepan with 1 cup of water; season lightly with salt and pepper. Bring to a boil and simmer, covered, over medium heat until the zucchini is slightly tender but still crunchy, about 2 minutes. Reserve without draining.

2 In a large skillet, heat the oil over high heat until hot but not quite smoking. Add the garlic and onion; sauté, stirring, until the onion is translucent, about 2 minutes. Add the tomato. Simmer until the water is partly evaporated, about 5 minutes. Add the corn and roasted poblanos and simmer 5 minutes more.

3 Add the zucchini and evaporated milk to the corn-chile mixture. Bring to a boil. Add the diced cheese and heat just until the cheese melts. Serve immediately.

Sopa Seca
("Dry" Soup)
≈ *Zarela Martinez* ≈
ZARELA RESTAURANT, NEW YORK

Neither dry nor a soup, sopa seca is actually a pilaf-style pasta browned in oil and then cooked like rice in water or broth until the liquid is absorbed. Zarela (pictured at right taking dinner orders as a child) ate this dish at her family's ranch in Chihuahua for lunch sprinkled with grated cheese. It's one of her comfort foods.

≈ KITCHEN MEMORIES ≈

My mother sent me to this cooking teacher in Los Angeles by the name of Lillian Haines who was a caterer as well as a cooking instructor, and she gave me a week-long private class on catering and setting up a business. She taught me the most important thing in my professional life. She said that I had to develop an identity, a particular cooking style, so unique that if people went to a party and tasted the food, they would say, "Oh, Zarela must be catering tonight." When I took that course, I didn't really know anything. I was just cooking from *Bon Appétit* and *Gourmet* for my customers in El Paso, because at that time, you know, Mexican food wasn't for parties, so I was doing international food. Very shortly thereafter I went to New Orleans to take a course called "The Enraged Chicken." It turned out to be a really bad course. My mom said, "Don't worry about it, we'll just go and eat in all the restaurants in town and then duplicate the food." We're both very good at that, we can both duplicate anything we taste. During that week we met Paul Prudhomme, and they sat me in front of him, and my mother kept saying to me, "Go talk to him," and I used to be very shy, and I said, "No mama," and she said, "GO TALK TO HIM!" in a way that only a mother can do, so I did, and I told him about my disappointment with the class I'd come to take and he said, "Well, why don't you come work with me and I'll teach you Cajun and you teach me Mexican." So I went in and worked with him for a week, and two months to the day later, I was cooking at Tavern on the Green for Paul because he was supposed to be doing an event and couldn't be there. It was a regional American buffet. Alice Waters came carrying her little lettuces and I came to do the Tex-Mex food. I was thirty-one.

1 large tomato
1 large jalapeño chili
1 small onion, coarsely chopped
1 large garlic clove
6 sprigs fresh cilantro
¼ cup vegetable oil
1 (7-ounce) package small shaped
    pasta such as midolline or alphabet
2 cups chicken stock or water
Shredded Parmesan, for garnish
Pico de gallo salsa, for garnish

1 Heat a heavy, ungreased griddle or cast-iron skillet over medium-low heat until a drop of water sizzles on contact. Place the tomato and jalapeño in the pan and cook, turning frequently, until the skins of the tomato and chili are blackened and blistered all over, about 15 minutes. Remove the tomato to a bowl to hold the juices. Place the chili in a small plastic or paper bag; let it rest for 10 minutes. When it is cool enough to handle, peel off the charred skin. If some tiny blackened bits remain, they will just add to the flavor. Be sure to save all the delicious juices.

2 Place the tomato, onion, garlic, cilantro, and jalapeño in a blender or food processor and process until almost smooth, about 1 minute. Reserve.

3 Place the oil in a small Dutch oven or medium saucepan; heat over medium-high heat, then add the pasta and cook, stirring constantly, until golden. Remove all but 2 tablespoons of the oil.

4 Add the puréed tomato mixture and cook, stirring often, for 2 minutes. Reduce the heat to low; add the chicken stock and bring to a simmer. Cover the Dutch oven and cook for 20 minutes, or until the liquid is absorbed.

5 Serve with shredded Parmesan and pico de gallo salsa if desired.

Mireille's Moroccan Salads
≈ *Lisa Schroeder* ≈
MOTHER'S BISTRO & BAR, PORTLAND, OREGON

Lisa's mother-in-law, Mireille, was born in Tangier and raised in Casablanca, Morocco. She taught Lisa the fundamentals of cooking, based on Moroccan and French cuisines. Most Moroccan meals start with an array of salads like the following, which are meant to be nibbled on while sipping aperitifs and chatting with family and friends. They are shared with lots of crusty French bread, which is great for soaking up the dressings and scooping up the salads. (Traditional Moroccans don't use cutlery—they eat with their fingers.) You could also eat these with toasted pita bread, in a more Middle Eastern style.

SALADE CUITE
COOKED SALAD OR TOMATO AND PEPPER JAM
SERVES 6

¼ cup extra virgin olive oil
8 cloves garlic, sliced thin
1 (28-ounce) can tomatoes,
   with juice

4 green bell peppers, roasted, peeled,
   seeded, and sliced
2 jalapeño or serrano peppers, roasted
   and peeled, but left whole

1 Heat a sauté pan over medium heat and add the olive oil and the garlic. Sauté the garlic until slightly soft, 3 to 5 minutes, making sure that it does not brown at all.

2 Add the tomatoes and peppers and bring to a boil. Cook over medium high heat, stirring occasionally, until most of the liquid has evaporated (about 30 minutes).

3 Lower the heat and continue to cook until virtually all moisture has evaporated, being sure to stir frequently with a rubber spatula so it does not scorch. There will be fewer and fewer bubbles, and you'll know it's done when there are virtually no bubbles of liquid when you stir the "jam." This can take as long as an hour. Cool and refrigerate. This can be made a week in advance, and stored in the refrigerator, traditionally with a thin layer of olive oil on top (this is optional). It's best served at room temperature.

MOROCCAN CHOPPED SALAD

SERVES 6

1 cucumber, peeled, seeded, and diced
   very small
½ green bell pepper, diced very small
2 tomatoes, diced very small
2 scallions, very finely chopped

¼ cup very finely shredded romaine,
   red, or green-leaf lettuce
Juice of 1 small lemon
¼ cup vegetable oil
Salt and freshly ground pepper to taste

Place all of ingredients in a mixing bowl and mix well with clean hands or tongs. This salad can be made a few hours ahead and refrigerated. Allow the salad to sit a room temperature for an hour or so before serving.

BEET OR CARROT SALAD

SERVES 6

2 cups beets (about 3 medium beets)
   or 2 cups carrots (about 4 carrots)
½ teaspoon ground cumin
½ teaspoon harissa (a hot red-pepper
   paste, available in gourmet or Middle
   Eastern food shops)

2 tablespoons extra virgin olive oil
Salt and freshly ground pepper to taste
1 tablespoon fresh lemon juice

1 If using beets, boil the beets whole in salted water until fork-tender, 30 to 45 minutes, depending on their size. Remove them from the pot and cool until they can be handled. Using a paring knife, peel them and either dice them into ½-inch cubes or slice them about ⅛ inch thick.

2 If using carrots, peel and slice them about ⅛ inch thick. Bring a pot of salted water to a boil and cook the carrots until fork-tender, about 7 minutes. Remove the carrots from pot and submerge them in a bath of ice water to stop the cooking. Strain the carrots and set aside.

3 In a mixing bowl, toss the carrots or beets with the cumin, harissa, olive oil, salt, pepper, and lemon juice. Refrigerate until 1 hour before serving. Before serving, remove from the refrigerator and allow the salad to come to room temperature. Can be made up to 2 days ahead.

Baduni
~ Cynthia Salvato ~
BOSTON UNIVERSITY, BOSTON

Cindy Salvato's Irish and French-Canadian mom was, in some ways, the typical 1960s and '70s cook—it was a time when "chili" was franks and beans and Jell-O was king. While those kinds of foods were certainly part of Cindy's culinary history, what distinguished her mother's cooking was her fondness for creating the traditional dishes Cindy's Italian father loved so much. Weekends were filled with Italian foods—meatballs, lasagna, pasta with lentils, and the ubiquitous Italian gravy. Growing up in Watertown, Massachusetts, Cindy was also surrounded by large Greek and Middle Eastern populations, and the different dishes of those cultures often showed up on the family table as well.

Over the years she has worked in a wide variety of places, including the Marriot at Copley Place, L'Espalier, Michela's, and Boston University where she teaches cooking. This unique recipe comes straight out of Cindy's culinary heritage and it has been passed down for several generations. Cindy told us: "For as long as I can remember, my Aunt Nancy has been creating and perfecting a dish that her Aunt Nancy made on New Year's Eve. Baduni is Sicilian in origin and is made from chicory, anchovies, and fresh plum tomatoes. My aunt Nancy taught me to make it the same way she remembers her aunt making it. Always enjoy this dish with coffee; I'm not sure why, it's just a great Salvato tradition."

⚜ KITCHEN MEMORIES ⚜

I cooked with my mom a lot. She was constantly learning the dishes that my dad grew up with. Around Christmas my mother would make fruitcakes and an enormous fruit salad. When it was fruit salad time, there would be twenty huge grapefruits looming and I'd always think, "Oh God, now she's going to want us to peel those grapefruits," because that was our job. After a while we grew to really enjoy doing it with her. Now we all make that fruit salad using the same recipe.

DOUGH
2 teaspoons active dry yeast
2 teaspoons sugar
2 tablespoons olive oil
3 cups all-purpose flour
2 teaspoons salt

FILLING
1¼ pounds fresh green-leafed chicory
    (radicchio is a red-leafed Italian
    chicory and can be substituted)
3 medium plum tomatoes
1 (2-ounce) can flat anchovies
Freshly ground pepper to taste
2 tablespoons olive oil for frying

1 For the dough: Whisk the yeast in 1¼ cups of water; set aside for 5 minutes. Blend in the remaining ingredients and knead by hand for 5 minutes. Transfer the dough to a lightly oiled bowl; cover with plastic wrap and place it in a warm place to rise for 1 hour.

2 For the filling: Trim the chicory and discard any old leaves; wash the leaves thoroughly in cold water and spin them dry in a salad spinner. Lay out the leaves on paper towels and roll them up to absorb any excess water. Slice the tomatoes and set them aside. Drain the anchovies and reserve the oil; set aside.

3 To assemble the baduni: Preheat the oven to 400° F. Lightly flour a 9-inch pie pan. Have ready a 12-inch Teflon-coated frying pan and a large dinner dish for turning out the baduni. Transfer the dough to a lightly floured work surface. Cut the dough in half and roll out each half into a 14-inch circle.

6 Line the pie pan with one circle of dough and pile the chicory leaves into the pan. The mound will be about 6-inches high. Grind fresh black pepper over the top of the leaves. Place the anchovies around, then sprinkle on the anchovy oil. Place the sliced tomatoes over the surface of the chicory. Lightly brush water around the edge of the dough; lay the second circle of dough over the top. With a fork, crimp the top and bottom together tightly. You are now ready to fry.

7 Heat the olive oil in the pan over medium heat. Transfer the baduni carefully to the pan and cook it for 3 to 4 minutes. Place a dinner plate over the top, and with one swift movement, holding the plate firmly, invert the baduni onto the dinner plate; slide it back to the pan and cook the other side for 3 minutes.

8 To bake it, place the pie pan over the top while it is still in the pan and again, invert it into the pie pan. The baduni itself will be large and will hang over the sides of the pan slightly. Bake for 15 minutes, until it is a rich golden brown.

Mother's Hearty Hungarian Goulash
Nora Pouillon
RESTAURANT NORA AND ASIA NORA, WASHINGTON, D.C.

Owner of the first and one of the only certified organic restaurants in America and a strong proponent of whole, unprocessed foods, Nora Pouillon (pictured with her daughters, below) would be something of a novelty today in her native Vienna, Austria, where fried foods and cold cuts are standard fare. The truth is that her family was a novelty even when she was a child growing up in Austria. Her father, described by Nora as a simple eater, loved fresh fruits and yogurt, and young Nora would look forward to his forays to the markets because he would return with what she thought of as "exotic" fruits like oranges, clementines, strawberries, and coconuts. During World War II, Nora's father even relocated his family to a farm so they could continue to have fresh, wholesome foods at a time when it would have been difficult to procure produce and fresh meats in their hometown. Her mother rarely fried anything, and when she did, would use peanut oil rather than the standard lard. This wonderful stew reflects Nora's Austrian heritage and continues to be a source of warm and comforting childhood memories for Nora.

SERVES 4 TO 6

5 tablespoons vegetable oil

6 large onions, sliced into rings

3 pounds beef, cut into ½-inch cubes

1½ tablespoons Hungarian sweet paprika

1 tablespoon caraway seeds

½ tablespoon dried marjoram

½ teaspoon cayenne

1 lemon, juiced and zested

Salt and pepper to taste

½ cup tomato paste, mixed with 1 cup of water or stock

Sour cream, for garnish

1 Preheat the oven to 350° F.

2 Heat the oil in a heavy, thick casserole or pot. Sauté the onion rings over low heat until soft, about 30 minutes.

3 Add the beef to the casserole and brown. Add the paprika, caraway seeds, marjoram, cayenne, lemon zest, lemon juice, salt, and pepper. Stir until spices develop an aroma.

4 Add the tomato paste mixed with water or stock. Use more water or stock if needed so that the liquid just covers all the meat.

5 Raise the heat under the pot and bring to a boil. Tightly cover the top with aluminum foil, then place the lid on. Place in the preheated oven.

6 Cook for 1 to 2 hours, until the meat is fork-tender. Serve in a bowl with boiled potatoes or bread dumplings. Add a dollop of sour cream if the goulash is very spicy. Enjoy!

Russian Salmon Pie
Kirsten Dixon

WINTERLAKE LODGE, REDOUBT BAY LODGE,
AND RIVERSONG LODGE, ALASKA

Kristen and her daughters Mandy and Carly (pictured opposite) have been making this dish at the lodge for more than twenty years. They get a little fancy these days and make the pies individually, and sometimes with more exotic "gourmet" ingredients, but this is the original version and is still Kirsten's favorite. Though the Dixon's heritage isn't necessarily Russian, their Alaskan cultural cuisine has a Russian influence and has been part of Mandy and Carly's cultural heritage since they were born.

⊰ KITCHEN MEMORIES ⊱

Obviously, I live in a specific regional locale—off the culinary map in the true sense. Alaska is isolated. There aren't many restaurants here—there aren't many people up here, period, but there are a lot of people in Alaska that are very educated about food. Alaska doesn't have a true Pacific Rim profile in the same sense that Seattle does—we have a little more Russian influence and a lot more Korean and Japanese influence. We also have a lot of Scandinavians who live here, and all of that swirls around and becomes what we call Alaskan Regional Cuisine. We have a lot of indigenous products that are unique to Alaska, such as reindeer and wild berries, and we have, although it's brief, the history of the Gold Rush and sourdough, like California. The majority of people living in Alaska live in an isolated way, so they have to deal with the struggles of procuring products. Many communities pay as much as a dollar a pound for getting freight out to their communities. Children going to public school above the Arctic Circle are never served fresh produce or fruit because it freezes on the runway, so everything served at school is from cans. So it's a challenge. There are wonderful aspects of living in a place that is so remote. Our air is clean, our water is pure, and we don't have polluted soils. We can grow organic here very easily. We have this funny mix of wonderful luxury living in a natural place combined with isolation and environmental harshness, and we've forged a cuisine and a culinary heritage that we call our own.

3 tablespoons unsalted butter
1 yellow onion, peeled and sliced into thin rings
2 sheets frozen puff pastry, thawed
1½ pounds Alaska salmon, cooked and flaked
2 cups cooked brown rice
½ cup shredded sharp Cheddar cheese

½ pound mushrooms, sliced
½ head green cabbage, shredded
½ cup fine bread crumbs
Salt and freshly ground pepper to taste
2 tablespoons minced fresh dill
1 hard-cooked egg, chopped
¼ cup heavy cream
1 egg, beaten

1 Preheat the oven to 375° F.

2 Melt the butter in a wide sauté pan over medium heat. Add the onion and sauté until softened, about 5 minutes. Remove from the pan and set aside.

3 Take one sheet of the puff pastry and roll it out into a 12-x-12-inch square on a lightly floured surface. Place it in a 10-inch, deep-dish pie pan, leaving the excess dough draped over the sides of the pie pan, then top with the salmon, the brown rice, and the cheese.

4 Mix together the onion, mushrooms, cabbage, and bread crumbs. Season the mixture with salt and pepper. Spread this mixture over the cheese. Sprinkle with dill and chopped hard-boiled egg. Pour the cream over the filling.

5 Roll out the remaining puff pastry on a lightly floured surface. Brush the rim of the pie with a little water. Place the pastry over the top of the pie. Cut small slits in the pastry to let the steam escape, trim the edges, and crimp with a fork. Brush the pastry with the beaten egg. Bake for 35 to 40 minutes, or until the pastry is golden.

Kreplach
Alison Awerbuch

ABIGAIL KIRSCH CULINARY PRODUCTIONS, TARRYTOWN, NEW YORK

Alison's Jewish roots come through in this kreplach recipe. Traditionally served the day before Jewish holidays like Yom Kippur, on Hashanah Rabba, or on Purim, kreplach most often are eaten in soup as dumplings and resemble Italian ravioli, but also can be served as a side dish, boiled or boiled and then fried.

SERVES 24

FILLING
Vegetable oil
2 large onions, cut into ¼-inch dice
3 cups ground, cooked brisket or
    roasted chuck roast
2 eggs
2 tablespoons matzo meal
Salt and pepper to taste

DOUGH
2 eggs
1⅓ cups all-purpose flour
2 teaspoons cold water
1 teaspoon salt

1 In a small amount of vegetable oil, sauté the onion over medium-high heat until translucent and let cool.

2 In a medium-sized mixing bowl, combine the cooked meat, eggs, matzo meal, salt, pepper, and cooked onion. Mix well. If the resulting mixture is dry and isn't holding together, add a little fat from the roast or some vegetable oil.

3 To make the dough, combine all of the dough ingredients and mix together with a fork until it forms a ball. Turn the dough out on a floured board and knead until smooth. Add more water if necessary. Roll the dough out to ⅛-inch thickness and cut into 2-inch squares.

4 Place a rounded teaspoon of meat filling on one-half of each square, then fold thedough over to form a triangle shape. Pinch the edges tight and let dry for ½ hour.

5 Boil 2 quarts of water with 2 tablespoons of salt and 2 tablespoons of oil. Drop in the kreplach, uncrowded, and cook for 12 minutes. Drain for a few minutes in a colander, then allow them to finish cooling on a cookie sheet. Repeat the cooking process until all the kreplach are cooked.

⊰ KITCHEN MEMORIES ⊱

I remember spending a lot of time with my one grandmother, a fabulous baker, although she never measured anything. She would make yeast cakes and yeast breads and would really just do it from memory. As I got a little older, I sat with her and would slow her down tremendously, because I would make her measure each thing as she went along so I could document everything so I would have recipes for myself, like this one, which I still have to this day. It was like I was putting handcuffs on her because she was used to just kind of getting an old jelly jar and putting some flour in it, and it was four jelly jars worth of flour and I'd have to put it into the measuring cup. Despite her annoyance at being slowed down, for me, these memories really evoke warm feelings about being with family.

```
                    KREPLACH
3 C Ground Brisket or Chuck Roast (Little Chicken)
      which has been roasted
2 Large sauted onions
2 Eggs
2 T Matza Meal
Salt - Pepper (Make a little spicy)
Mix all together.  If dry add a little fat gravy
from roast.

Dough:
2 Eggs                  2 Tsp. Cold Water
1-1/3 C Flour           1 Tsp. Salt
Turn on floured board and knead until smooth.
Add more water if necessary.
Roll out thin.  Cut in 2" squares.
Fill.  Pinch edges tight.
Dry for 1/2 hour.
Boil 2 Qts water with 2 T Salt and 2 T Oil
Drop  in Kreplach, uncrowded, and cook for
12 minutes.
Drain a few minutes in collander and cool
on cookie sheet.
```

Mom's Secret Kreplach can be parboiled and frozen or refrigerated for later use. Use sheets of wax or parchment paper to stack the dumplings in layers so they don't stick together.

⊰ KITCHEN MEMORIES ⊱

When I think about my favorite things from childhood, I remember that I always had this passion for vegetables—my friends would have their M&Ms, and I'd have whatever vegetable I was drawn to. My mom's parents came from Sicily, both from farm families, so there was a rich tradition of food from the land and very simple everyday cooking that focused a lot on seasonal vegetables. That's probably part of what still rings true for me when I think back. My grandfather turned my family's backyard in central New Jersey into a huge garden. There were five or six peach trees and rows and rows of all types of vegetables. His little matchbox of a garden—a small plot of land behind their three-story brownstone in Brooklyn—had fig trees and grapevines, and they always made their own wine. I remember the buckets of peaches that my grandmother (pictured, opposite, with my sister) and I would turn into peach pie or preserves or jam. I have a strong memory of the vegetables there, and an equally strong memory of making things by hand. It was about cooking by the senses—touching and smelling and looking at something and that's how Grandmom taught me. We never measured anything. When she would come on Fridays, oftentimes it would be pizza night, and we were all able to ask whomever we wanted to come. It would start early in the morning with a 5-pound bag of flour and in she taught me what to do by showing me what the dough should feel and like. I have notes that I took as a kid from learning by her side and that left a big impression.

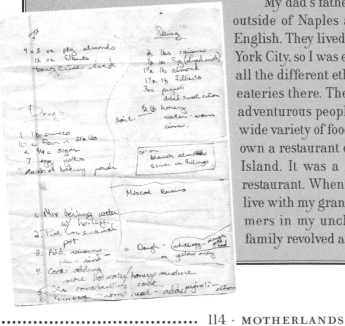

My dad's father was also Italian but from outside of Naples and my grandmother was English. They lived on Restaurant Row in New York City, so I was exposed to a rich tradition of all the different ethnicities represented in the eateries there. They were real explorers and adventurous people who enjoyed sampling a wide variety of foods. My uncle even went on to own a restaurant on the North Shore of Long Island. It was a *New York Times* three-star restaurant. When I was a kid I would go and live with my grandmother and work for summers in my uncle's restaurant. Our whole family revolved around food.

Mashed Carrots and Rutabaga
❧ *Elizabeth Germain* ❧

Elizabeth Germain's English great-aunt passed this recipe down, and her family continues the tradition of using rutabagas. Elizabeth says, "Often labeled 'yellow turnips' or 'waxed turnips,' rutabagas are related to turnips but are sweet instead of peppery. This humble dish is easy to prepare and praised for its sweet, earthy flavor, comforting texture, and brilliant orange color."

SERVES 4

1 medium rutabaga (about 1¼ pounds),
    peeled and cut into 1-inch chunks
8 medium carrots (about 1¼ pounds),
    peeled and cut into 1-inch chunks

Salt to taste
4 tablespoons (½ stick) unsalted butter,
    softened and cut into 4 pieces
Freshly ground pepper as needed

1 Place the rutabaga and carrot chunks in a large saucepan and add water to cover by 2 inches. Add a generous amount of salt and bring to a boil over high heat. Reduce the heat to medium and cook until the vegetables are very tender, 20 to 25 minutes. Drain the carrots and turnips.

2 Return the vegetables to the empty saucepan and place over low heat. Stir constantly with a wooden spoon to remove excess moisture, 1 to 2 minutes.

3 Remove the pan from the heat and add the butter. Use a potato masher to turn the carrots and turnips into a chunky mash. Season to taste with salt and pepper. Serve immediately.

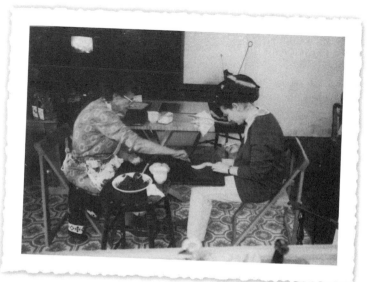

Auntie Beth's Chicken Paprikash
❧ *Anita Lo* ❧
ANNISA, NEW YORK

Anita Lo (pictured with her grandmother and sister, below) says she grew up in a "food-obsessed household." Though they lived in Michigan, Anita and her family traveled a lot and were exposed to the foods of their mother's Chinese-Malaysian heritage as well as the cuisines of their multicultural nannies, especially one Hungarian nanny, whom Anita fondly refers to as "Auntie Beth."

Anita first became interested in cooking when, during her pursuit of a degree in French literature, she went to study in Paris and was inspired by her sister to take a class at La Varenne cooking school. She thought the language practice would serve her well educationally and discovered she liked cooking so much that when she graduated from college, she sought out a restaurant job. She found what she was looking for at Bouley in Manhattan and became so enamored of the restaurant business that she decided to return to France, where she received a degree from the Ritz Escoffier school. Chanterelle, also in New York City, was next on Anita's whirlwind culinary adventure, and after a sojourn in Asia, Anita returned to Manhattan to take her first chef position at Can, a French-Vietnamese restaurant in SoHo. Two restaurant jobs later, in 2000, she undertook to open her own place, Annisa, and has since been named one of the top ten "Best New Chefs in America" by *Food and Wine* magazine as well as "Best New Restaurant Chef" by the *Village Voice*.

Though her restaurant's cuisine is upscale contemporary American, Anita still finds comfort in the humble home cooking of her past. This recipe for Chicken Paprikash remains one of her favorites to this day.

8 chicken thighs, trimmed of excess fat

3 tablespoons sweet Hungarian paprika

Salt and pepper to taste

3 tablespoons flavorless vegetable oil
   (canola or corn, for example)

1 large onion, chopped

1 cup sour cream

3 tablespoons all-purpose flour, sifted

1 pound egg noodles, cooked

2 tablespoons chopped fresh parsley

1 Mix the chicken thighs with the paprika and season both sides with salt and pepper.

2 Place a pot over medium-high heat; add the oil, then the onion. Reduce the heat and cook until translucent. Add the chicken pieces and turn over to coat with the oil. Cover with water and return to simmer and cook for 20 minutes.

3 Mix the sour cream and flour together. Add to the chicken pot and stir. Boil hard for about 5 minutes while stirring to break up any lumps. If you want a thicker sauce, add more flour and boil again. Check the seasoning and adjust salt and pepper as needed and serve over hot egg noodles. Garnish with chopped parsley.

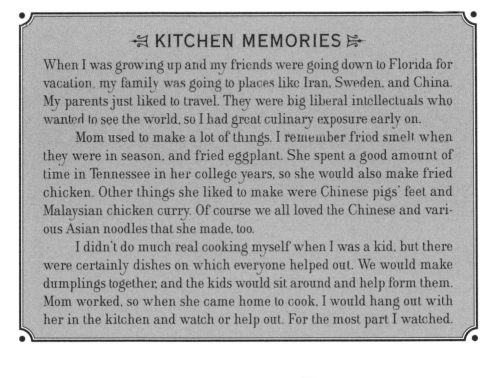

⊰ KITCHEN MEMORIES ⊱

When I was growing up and my friends were going down to Florida for vacation, my family was going to places like Iran, Sweden, and China. My parents just liked to travel. They were big liberal intellectuals who wanted to see the world, so I had great culinary exposure early on.

Mom used to make a lot of things. I remember fried smelt when they were in season, and fried eggplant. She spent a good amount of time in Tennessee in her college years, so she would also make fried chicken. Other things she liked to make were Chinese pigs' feet and Malaysian chicken curry. Of course we all loved the Chinese and various Asian noodles that she made, too.

I didn't do much real cooking myself when I was a kid, but there were certainly dishes on which everyone helped out. We would make dumplings together, and the kids would sit around and help form them. Mom worked, so when she came home to cook, I would hang out with her in the kitchen and watch or help out. For the most part I watched.

Chile Verde
❧ *Traci Des Jardins* ❧
JARDINIERE, ACME CHOPHOUSE, AND MIJITA, SAN FRANCISCO

Traci Des Jardins, now a successful restaurant owner in San Francisco, was a self-described "avid home cook" as a child growing up in the central valley of California. She attributes her early passion for cooking to boredom and her mother's subscriptions to *Gourmet* and *Bon Appétit*. Like most children who get involved in the kitchen early, Traci started out baking, but by the time she was ten or eleven, she was undertaking ambitious savory dishes. Though she describes her early cooking as a hobby, she also acknowledges that food was the center of her family's universe when she was growing up.

Her maternal grandparents were from Mexico, and they loved to make the traditional dishes of their homeland. Traci remembers their cooking everything from menudo to tortillas and tamales. Her dad's father was from Louisiana, and his cooking had Cajun roots. His fiery shrimp creole, crawdad boils, and outdoor grilling were cooled and balanced by the wonderful baked goods his Swedish-and-Norwegian wife, Traci's grandmother, prepared regularly. Having graduated from high school at sixteen, Traci floundered in her first year of college. Realizing she was too young to be there, she decided that she would like to pursue the two things she was passionate about—cooking and skiing. Fortunately her aunt and uncle were friends with Joachim Splicha, acknowledged in 1991 as James Beard's Best California Chef and a continuing presence on the California restaurant scene. When she told them what she wanted to do, they put her in touch with him and he invited her to work with him. She did, and was so inspired by the work she was doing that she didn't ski for the next thirteen years.

Trained by the best of the best (Alain Ducasse, Pierre and Michel Troisgros, Alain Passard, and Lucas Carton, among others) Traci is now the mother of son Eli and owns and operates three restaurants: Jardiniere, Acme Chop House, and, perhaps the nearest to her heart and heritage, an upscale taqueria, Mijita, whose name means "little daughter."

4 pounds pork butt (shoulder)

2 pounds tomatillos, husks removed

1 pound Anaheim or poblano chiles
(green peppers may be substituted)

2 yellow onions, peeled

6 cloves garlic

1 bunch cilantro, washed

Salt and pepper to taste

All-purpose flour as needed

2 tablespoons vegetable oil

1 teaspoon ground cumin

½ teaspoon dried oregano

1 Cut the meat into 1½-inch cubes. Cut the tomatillos into quarters, cut the chilies into 1-inch pieces, chop the onions into 1-inch pieces, and peel the garlic and chop it roughly. Remove the large stems from the cilantro and chop it roughly. Lay the meat out on a tray, sprinkle generously with salt, pepper, and flour, and toss until coated.

2 Place a heavy skillet on the stove over medium-high heat. When hot, add the oil and fry the pork until golden brown on all sides. Remove the meat from the pan and add the vegetables. Cook over low heat until soft, add the meat, spices, and herbs to the pan, cover just to the top of the meat with water, and bring to a simmer. Simmer for 2 hours, or until the pork is tender. Serve with warm tortillas, if desired.

⊰ KITCHEN MEMORIES ⊱

My dad was a rice farmer in the central valley. He still farms a little bit of rice. That was really the only food crop that he grew. He occasionally grew sugar beets and cotton, but we always had and ate rice. There weren't any good bakeries around, so there wasn't any good fresh bread, and there weren't really any potatoes, either. Rice was our staple, and to this day it's my favorite.

My father never wanted us to follow in his footsteps. He could see sort of the end in sight, which is indeed what has happened. He farmed between 3,000 and 5,000 acres, and my parents aren't in great shape financially. They've just been hanging on by a thread for fifteen years. And that's not going to change. The future of farming isn't great. But my son Eli has said he wants to be a farmer, and I have to admit, if he grew up to be a farmer, I'd be thrilled because it's such an important role in the world.

Grandma Salazar's Albondigas Soup
Traci Des Jardins

JARDINIERE, ACME CHOP HOUSE, AND MIJITA, SAN FRANCISCO

SERVES 6 TO 8

½ cup short-grain white rice

2 white onions, peeled and diced

Vegetable oil as needed

½ pound ground pork

½ pound ground beef

2 eggs

1 bunch cilantro, chopped

1 teaspoon ground cumin

1 tablespoon dried oregano

Salt and pepper to taste

1 clove garlic, peeled, and finely minced

1 rib celery, diced

1 carrot, peeled and diced

½ pound tomatoes, blanched, peeled, and diced, or 1 (12-ounce) can peeled and crushed tomatoes

4 cups chicken stock

2 sprigs mint leaves, chopped

1 medium zucchini, diced

1 Bring 1 cup of water to a boil and pour over the rice; let soak for 20 minutes, then drain.

2 Sweat half of the onion in scant vegetable oil until soft, let cool, and then add to the meat. Add the soaked rice, egg, one-half of the cilantro, the cumin, oregano, and salt and pepper to taste. Blend everything together very well and form into 1-inch meatballs.

3 In a large sauté pan over medium-high, heat 2 tablespoons of oil and brown the meatballs lightly. Remove from the pan and add the remaining onion, garlic, celery, and carrots; sweat slightly and add the tomato. Add the chicken stock and bring to a simmer; add the meatballs and the mint. Simmer for about 1 hour; season to taste with salt and pepper. Add the zucchini and cook for another 10 minutes. Garnish with the remaining cilantro and serve.

Pork Coated with Anise-Scented Roasted Rice over Sweet Potatoes
Olivia Wu

Olivia Wu (pictured with her mother, page 123) grew up in Thailand, which she describes as one of the most "abundant places on earth." Known as the "rice bowl of Asia," Thailand produces as much as three crops of rice during one rainy season. Fruits and vegetables burst with flavor (one of Olivia's friends says that fruit from Thailand makes fruit from other countries taste like "cooking fruit"), and fish is everywhere. Her mother didn't cook, but was Olivia's primary teacher because every morning at breakfast, she and the family cook would sit down together and discuss, in great detail, what the meals of the day would include. Olivia learned by osmosis.

When she arrived in the United States to attend university, she became very homesick and began cooking to alleviate her yearning for home. Her friends, both European and Asian, clamored for more, and her letters home became increasingly food-focused. The more she cooked, the more questions she had for her mother.

After graduate school and marriage, she began throwing dinner parties for friends who couldn't believe that they were eating Chinese food—it was so different from what they were used to getting at their local take-out counter. Before she knew what was happening, Olivia was teaching cooking classes.

While she was at home with the baby, in fact, right after he was born, she was approached by a publisher to write a book. He convinced her to do it based on the fact that "babies sleep all the time anyway." Olivia now says that it took her about three or four years to recover from that project! The book, *The Grand Wok,* won a Tastemaker Award (now called the James Beard Award). Olivia loved the process of writing and when she and her husband divorced she applied for a newspaper job at the *Chicago Daily Herald* and was hired. Later she took a job at *Chicago Sun Times* and worked as a journalist in Chicago for a total of twelve years before finally moving to California where she remains today.

Mom's Secret Glutinous rice is short-grain rice with a higher starch content than long- or medium-grain rice, causing it to stick together when cooked.

PORK

½ **pound pork belly without skin or well-marbled Boston butt, sliced ¼ inch thick**

3 **tablespoons light soy sauce**

1 **tablespoon mushroom soy sauce**

⅓ **cup Shaoxing (or other) rice wine**

½ **star anise**

½ **cassia or cinnamon stick**

RICE

1 **cup white rice**

1 **cup white glutinous rice**

½ **star anise**

½ **cassia or cinnamon stick**

1 **pound sweet potatoes, peeled and cut into ¾-inch slices**

½ **cup dark or light brown sugar**

1 *The day before,* place the pork with seasonings and spices in a bowl and combine well. Refrigerate overnight.

2 Preheat the oven to 350° F. Place the two rices, anise, and cassia or cinnamon on a cookie tray and roast until toasty brown, stirring often. This will take from 30 to 45 minutes. Alternately, you may stir-fry the rice ingredients in a dry wok, the traditional Chinese way. The rice may be roasted up to a week ahead.

3 To assemble: Bring the pork to room temperature. Grind the roasted rice and spices in a clean coffee grinder or food processor to a fine or medium crumb (I prefer a medium crumb). Pour the ground rice mixture on a sheet of wax paper. Coat each slice of pork with the crumbs and fill a 9x5x3-inch loaf pan (or two 6-inch heat-proof bowls) with the slices in an attractive pattern. Place in a Chinese tiered metal steamer or in a wok set up to steam with plenty of boiling water and a domed lid *(see note)*. Steam over high heat for 30 minutes. Place the sweet-potato slices over the meat and sprinkle with brown sugar. Adjust the heat to medium and

cook, adding boiling water whenever necessary, for another 2 hours. The dish is done when a chopstick slips easily into the pork.

4 Invert onto a serving plate and serve immediately. You may wish to ring the mold with quickly stir-fried vegetables such as spinach or amaranth greens.

Mom's Secret To steam food in a wok you'll need a steamer rack and a domed lid for your wok. Fill the bottom of the wok to within 1 inch of the bottom of the steamer rack. Place the food in the bowls or loaf pan onto the rack. Cover with domed lid and bring to a boil. Steam for the suggested amount of time, replacing water in the wok as needed. The same can be done in a covered Dutch oven fitted with a round wire rack.

⊰ KITCHEN MEMORIES ⊱

Growing up in Thailand, and especially in Bangkok, meant growing up in probably one of the most abundant places on earth. Fish just jumps from the river. We lived in the city and even then, the Thai servants could drop a line in the river and catch a fish overnight for their favorite catfish stew. Construction workers could just, for lunchtime, walk a few hundred yards, get a couple of pinches of things from nearby bushes—water spinach or mimosa—and right in the middle of this construction site they'd build a fire and cook dinner. The earth and waters were just incredibly abundant. On top of that, Bangkok was really a very sophisticated city. It was our custom, for maybe a year or two, to go for Kobe steaks at the Japanese restaurant every Saturday. We had Danish smorgasbord, French food, and some of the best Chinese food I've ever had. The cosmopolitan eating scene was all right there. As in much of Thailand, there was a tremendous juxtaposition of abundance and poverty, but without a doubt the land was very giving. It was a wonderful, wonderful place to grow up with food.

Because I'm an immigrant and had my roots kind of ripped out from under me when I moved to the United States, I have had to really think hard about where home is on this earth. A result of this long journey, which is still going on, is that home is wherever I am and that there must be a spiritual connection and that spiritual connection is very often through food.

Chocolate-Almond Cake with Chocolate Glaze
❧ *Nora Pouillon* ❧
RESTAURANT NORA AND ASIA NORA, WASHINGTON, D.C.

Nora Pouillon grew up in Austria, which is famous for its wonderful (and extremely fattening!) pastries and desserts. This cake recipe was passed down to Nora by her grandmother. She describes it as "intense and very Austrian."

SERVES 12

CAKE
1½ cups raw almonds
4 ounces (1 stick) unsalted butter
4 ounces semisweet or bittersweet
   chocolate
¾ cup sugar
6 eggs, separated
½ cup bread crumbs

CHOCOLATE GLAZE
3 ounces semisweet or bittersweet
   chocolate
3 ounces unsalted butter, softened
1 ounce milk chocolate at room
   temperature, for garnish
Whipped cream (optional)

1 Preheat the oven to 325° F.

2 Grind the almonds in a mini-chopper or food processor until fine.

3 Butter an 8-inch springform with about a teaspoon of the butter and dust with flour or some of the bread crumbs.

4 Soften the chocolate in a double boiler over simmering water or in the microwave. Remove from the heat and allow to cool.

5 Combine the butter, sugar, and softened chocolate in the bowl of a mixer and whip until the batter changes to a lighter color and becomes creamy, about 5 minutes. Scrape down the sides of the bowl once or twice while whipping. Add the egg yolks, one at a time, continuing to beat. Lower the speed of the mixer and add the ground almonds and bread crumbs.

6 In a separate bowl, beat the egg whites until they are soft but not stiff. Stir a third of the beaten whites into the batter, blending thoroughly. Gently fold in the remaining whites, working quickly and carefully to incorporate all the whites without deflating the batter.

7 Pour the batter into the prepared pan and smooth the top. Bake for 50 to 55 minutes, or until a toothpick inserted in the center comes out clean.

8 Allow the cake to cool in the pan for 10 minutes before turning it out onto a cake rack. Let the cake cool completely before glazing it.

9 Melt the chocolate in a double boiler over simmering water or in the microwave on 50 per cent power in 10 second increments to avoid burning. Add the butter and stir until blended and smooth. Remove the glaze from the heat and allow it to cool and thicken to the consistency of thick cream.

10 Assemble the cake: Brush the cake to remove any loose crumbs, and place both the cake and the cooling rack on a sheet pan to catch the glaze. Slowly pour a pool of chocolate glaze over the center of the cake. Working from the center out, use a long metal spatula to spread the glaze evenly over the top and sides of the cake.

11 For a smoother look, glaze the cake a second time (optional). Scoop up the excess glaze from the sheet pan and reheat it in a small double boiler. Pour it through a sieve, if necessary, to remove any cake crumbs, and cool it slightly to thicken a bit. Pour the glaze again over the center of the top and allow it to spread without using a spatula.

12 With a vegetable peeler, shave off some curls of the milk chocolate and sprinkle them on top of the cake. Allow the glaze to set for about 2 hours at room temperature or 20 minutes in the refrigerator.

13 Serve with whipped cream, if desired.

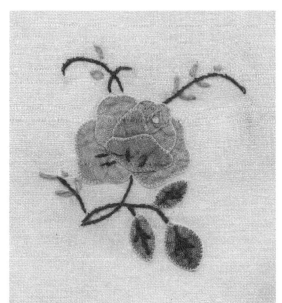

Baba's Mak

POPPY SEED STRUDEL

Dorothy Hamilton

THE FRENCH CULINARY INSTITUTE, NEW YORK

Every year at Christmastime Dorothy Hamilton's daughter Olivia (pictured with Dorothy, opposite), begs her to make this Czechoslovakian strudel. Their Christmas dinner is actually quite multicultural and includes lobster consommé, prime rib, chicken, and a bûche de noël. It is reflective of their own heritage as well as those of their family and friends.

MAKES 2 STRUDELS

DOUGH
2 packages active dry yeast
½ cup warm water
4½ cups all-purpose flour
¾ cup sugar
½ teaspoon salt
½ cup unsalted butter
2 large eggs
2 large egg yolks
½ cup sour cream

FILLING
1½ pounds ground poppy seed paste
  (see note)
½ cup milk
¼ cup honey
½ cup raisins softened in warm rum
1 cup sugar

ICING
1 cup confectioners' sugar
2 tablespoons fresh lemon juice

1 Soften the yeast in the warm water

2 Mix the flour, sugar, and salt. Cut the butter into small pieces and mix into the flour with a pastry blender or two knives until the mixture has a fine, even crumb.

3 Beat the eggs, egg yolks, and sour cream together; mix with the yeast, and then stir into the flour mixture.

4 Knead the dough on a floured surface for 5 to 10 minutes. The dough should start to have a sheen. Divide it in half. Put each half in greased bowls and cover to let rise in a warm place.

5 Prepare the filling: Soften the poppy seed paste with the milk. Keep adding milk until the paste becomes spreadable. Add the honey, raisins, and sugar.

6 Prepare two baking sheets by greasing them with butter or spraying with cooking spray. When the dough has risen to nearly double its bulk, roll it out into two large rectangles (each about 9 x 13 inches, ¼ inch thick) on a floured surface. (Depending on the size of your work space, you may need to do this in two batches.)

Mom's Secret Ground poppy seed paste is available in cans in some supermarkets in the baking section. You may also find it in Indian or Eastern European food shops. You can also prepare it yourself by grinding lightly toasted poppy seeds in a coffee or spice grinder in batches. You may want to add a tablespoon or so of confectioners' sugar before grinding to prevent the seeds from becoming oily.

7 Spread the poppy mixture on the dough, leaving a 1-inch border all around. (The poppy seeds will spread as you roll up the dough.) Roll the dough up into a log. Fold over the two ends of the log to seal in the poppy seeds.

8 Place on the prepared baking sheets. Cover. Let rise again until double in bulk (about 1½ hours). Preheat oven to 350° F.

9 Bake for about 45 minutes or until browned. (Check after 30 minutes.)

10 Cool the strudels completely before icing. To prepare the icing, blend the sugar and lemon juice until smooth. Spread over the rolls.

Aunt Emily's Kolacky
BOHEMIAN PASTRY COOKIES
Gwen Kvavli Gulliksen

Gwen Gulliksen's (pictured opposite) aunts, June, Emily, and Bheula, as well as her mother, had a tremendous influence on her early culinary development. This is one of Gwen's Aunt Emily's famous Czechoslovakian recipes.

MAKES 2 DOZEN COOKIES

1 ounce cream cheese

1 ounce margarine

1 cup all-purpose flour

1 tablespoon sugar

1 teaspoon baking powder

1 teaspoon salt

2 eggs, well beaten

Apricot jam, prune preserves, poppy seeds, or cottage cheese, as needed, for filling

Confectioners' sugar for dusting

1 Preheat the oven to 400° F.

2 Cream the cream cheese and margarine together.

3 Sift the flour, sugar, baking powder, and salt together and blend into the cream cheese mixture. Add the eggs and stir to blend.

4 Chill for at least 30 minutes in the refrigerator, and then roll the dough out on a floured surface to 1/2-inch thickness.

5 Using a round cutter about 1½ inches in diameter, cut out the cookies and place them on an ungreased cookie sheet. Using three fingers, make an indentation in the center of each cookie and fill with a teaspoon of apricot jam, prune preserves, poppy seeds, or cottage cheese. (These are traditional Czech fillings for these cookies, but substitutions can certainly be made.)

6 Bake for 15 minutes. When slightly cooled, remove from the baking sheet. When fully cooled, dust with confectioners' sugar.

⚔ KITCHEN MEMORIES ⚔

My Aunt Emily was Czechoslovakian, and she always had amazing dumplings and two meats for all of the dinner parties, kolacky cookies, sweet-and-sour cabbage, and just lots of great things. She passed away a few years ago, but she was so proud of her recipes and heritage that she placed an ad in the back of *Gourmet* magazine to sell her recipes for a dollar. This was almost 30 years ago. I found a group of those that were almost illegible because the ink was faded. She actually did sell some! Along with my other aunts, she really taught me how to cook.

Chapter Five
Celebrations

MUSEUMS AROUND THE WORLD are filled with ceremonial vessels—goblets, bowls, baskets, even cookware—that provide evidence of the importance of food in human culture. Today our lives are filled with traditions and ceremonies celebrated with food that are unique to a particular culture, a religion, or even a single family. Christmas and Easter, Hanukkah and Passover, Thanksgiving, birthdays, anniversaries, weddings, baptisms, graduations: All inspire us to spend hours, even days, working to prepare the perfect meal. These feasts continue to inspire generations of families to come together, setting aside the hectic pace of contemporary life, if even only for a day, to celebrate with food. It is during these times that culinary traditions (and the occasional pot or pan) are made or passed down.

We hope this chapter, which includes everything from Dina Altieri's Antipasti recipe to Barbara Sanders's family's traditional Christmas Bread, will inspire you to create and preserve family food traditions, no matter how modest or extravagant, because it is during these special times in our lives that the gift of love is so effortlessly expressed around a table surrounded by family.

Antipasti
⪼ Dina Altieri ⪻

NEW ENGLAND CULINARY INSTITUTE, ESSEX JUNCTION, VERMONT

Dina happened upon the professional culinary world quite by accident. As a teenager she started out as a paper girl with aspirations to be "a rock star, a dancer, and a comedian." The newspaper job helped her to earn enough money to buy a car, which in turn afforded her the opportunity to look for more gainful employment. After weeks of scouring the want-ads in her local paper she finally found a job in a brand new mall in Danbury, Connecticut—and what could make a teenager happier than more time in the mall! The place she settled on just happened to be a bakery. It was there that she fell in love with professional foodservice—in part because at work, behind the scenes, she could sing, dance, and crack jokes to her heart's content. And then, of course, she grew to love the work itself. A friend encouraged her to attend the Culinary Institute of America, and after graduation Dina honed her craft in a variety of restaurants from Virginia to California, where she eventually settled into a teaching job at the Cordon Bleu school. She watched the school grow from 80 students to more than 1,200 in her five years there before she moved on to teach at the New England Culinary Institute in Essex Junction, Vermont, where she continues to teach today.

SERVES 6 TO 8

GARLIC BREAD
1 loaf Italian bread
½ pound (2 sticks) unsalted butter
4 cloves garlic, minced
1 teaspoon salt
1 teaspoon black pepper
1 tablespoon dried basil
1 tablespoon dried oregano
1 tablespoon dried Italian parsley
3 tablespoons grated Parmesan cheese

ANTIPASTI
½ pound aged provolone cheese
½ pound fresh mozzarella cheese
½ pound salami
½ pound capocollo or pancetta
½ pound proscuitto
1 cup canned artichoke hearts
1 cup canned roasted red peppers
½ cup canned black olives
½ cup canned pepperoncini
12 canned anchovies, oil reserved

⊰ KITCHEN MEMORIES ⊱

My first recollection of cooking with my grandmother is building the antipasti platters. Typically I would see my grandmother at the holidays, any major holiday, like Christmas, Thanksgiving, or Easter and the antipasti would be the big precursor to the pasta course, and then there would be the meat course and, of course, dessert. It was a big to-do around the holiday time. We would roll the salami, the prosciutto, and the capocollo, and then we'd lay it out with the cheese and everything else. I got pretty good at it and knew where to put everything on the platter, and I did it the same way every year.

1 Preheat the oven to 350° F.

2 Prepare the garlic bread by gently slicing the loaf of bread lengthwise so that it is nearly split in half but still connected in the middle so the sides hold together. Combine the butter with the garlic over a gentle heat and spread the warm garlic butter onto each half of the bread.

3 Season each half with salt, black pepper, basil, oregano, parsley, and Parmesan. Place the loaf back together again and slice three-quarters of the way through the bread widthwise to create six to eight slices.

4 Wrap the loaf in aluminum foil and bake for 20 minutes. While the bread is in the oven, assemble the antipasti platter.

5 Cut the provolone and mozzarella into slices.

6 Roll the salami, capocollo, and prosciutto and begin layering each of the meats alternately to form a spiral shape on the bottom of the platter. Place the sliced cheeses around the platter or on top of the layered meats.

7 Place the artichoke hearts into a small bowl fitted in the center of the platter.

8 Slice the roasted red peppers into strips and lay the strips on top of the layered meats and cheeses to form a symmetrical design.

9 Follow with the olives, pepperoncini, and anchovies. Finish by drizzling the oil from the anchovy tin on top of the entire platter as a dressing.

10 Serve with warm garlic bread as a first course.

Balsamic Green Beans
❧ Deann and Lanie Bayless ❧
FRONTERA GRILL AND TOPOLOBAMPO, CHICAGO

Deann Bayless's daughter, Lanie, literally grew up in a room above the kitchen of the famed Frontera Grill. At age thirteen she is already very proficient in the kitchen, has an expansive palate, and has finished a cookbook with her father. This dish is a Thanksgiving tradition in the Bayless household, and it is one of Lanie's favorites.

About it she says, "These were the first vegetables I actually wanted to eat. (Unless you count Caesar Salad.) We make them every year at Thanksgiving, and I'm in charge of d-r-i-b-b-l-i-n-g on the balsamic vinegar. That's what they did when we ate at this inn in Italy. So it's what we do. Balsamic is expensive—so we dribble."

SERVES 4

Salt as needed

4 cups green beans, cleaned, stems and tips removed

2 tablespoons olive oil

1 large garlic clove, peeled

1½ to 2 teaspoons balsamic vinegar

1 In a large saucepan, bring 4 inches of water to boil over high heat. Add 2 teaspoons of salt. Add the green beans and cook for 7 minutes (5 minutes for the little French green beans). Drain and spread out on a large plate to cool.

2 Pour the oil into a large skillet. Set over medium heat. Crush the garlic through a garlic press into the oil. Add the green beans and cook for 3 or 4 minutes, stirring continuously, until the beans are hot. Sprinkle with about ¼ teaspoon salt. Stir to season evenly. Scoop onto a platter. Slowly and evenly pour the vinegar over the beans. Serve right away.

Mom's Secret The green beans can be regular ones, yellow ones, the skinny little French ones called haricot verts. Or they can be snow peas or sugar snap peas. Everyday balsamic vinegar is available in the grocery store, but you can find very special "artisanal" balsamic in specialty stores. Some of it is so expensive you want to call it black gold.

Roast Goose with Chestnuts and Wild Mushrooms
❧ *Anne Willan* ❧

Throughout the years Anne Willan (pictured on page 137) has maintained her English family's tradition of Christmas Goose, but she's added some accompaniments that reflect the nomadic nature of her life. Because Minnesota is one of her favorite places to visit, she might serve American wild rice, or as a gesture toward her son Simon's current place of employment, kasha from Russia. The gravy is always a "traditional French jus, dark and concentrated, without thickening." If you're looking to try something different from the traditional Christmas ham or turkey, Anne Willan's Christmas Goose is an excellent choice!

Mom's Secret Instead of stuffing, which tends to stew and steam inside a bird, try this with plain onions, roasted until they are caramelized and almost black. Rather than adding them to the goose, cook them separately so they are easier to control.

⊰ KITCHEN MEMORIES ⊱

It was a Burgundian farmer, Madame Fournillon, who gave me this recipe for goose which puts the chestnuts from our avenue of trees to good use with wild mushrooms from the market. Goose, like duck, is a bony bird and does not go far. You can generally count on one bird to serve six to eight, although our family of four has been known to strip the carcass at one sitting. At Christmas the type of wild mushrooms available varies and I often mix them, aiming for a contrast of color with black trumpets, golden girolles, and white sheep's feet or oyster mushrooms.

SERVES 6 TO 8

1 goose, about 10 pounds, with giblets
1 onion, peeled and sliced
1 carrot, peeled and sliced ¼ inch
2 tablespoons unsalted butter, softened
Salt and pepper to taste
2 pounds fresh chestnuts
2 cups milk, more if needed
2 cups veal or chicken stock
Trussing needle and string

FOR THE MUSHROOMS
1½ pounds wild mushrooms
½ cup (1 stick) butter
2 shallots, very finely chopped
1 clove garlic, finely chopped
2 tablespoons finely chopped fresh
  parsley

1 Preheat the oven to 450° F. Truss the goose using a trussing needle and set it on its back in a large roasting pan. Scatter the sliced onion, carrot, and the giblets around the bird (reserve the liver for another use or discard). Spread the bird with the softened butter and sprinkle it with salt and pepper.

2 Place the goose in the oven and roast, basting occasionally, until it is golden brown, about 40 minutes. Prick the bird all over with a fork to release fat under the skin. Lower the oven heat to 350° F, and continue roasting, basting, and pouring off the excess fat from the pan, for 2 to 2½ hours. Reserve the fat when you remove it from the pan.

3 Meanwhile, cook the chestnuts: Poke a hole in each chestnut with the point of a knife, put them in a pan of cold water, bring to a boil, and simmer for 2 minutes. Remove from the heat but leave the chestnuts in the water. Lift out a few chestnuts at a time on a draining spoon, let them cool slightly, and then strip off the skin and peel. Continue with the rest. Alternatively, you can strip off the skin and peel with a knife. Either way, this is a tiresome job, but once a year it's worth it.

4 Put the peeled chestnuts in a pan with enough milk to cover and add the lid. Bring them to a boil and simmer until almost tender, 15 to 20 minutes. You don't want the chestnuts too soft, or they will fall apart when roasted. Put 2 to 3 table-spoons of the reserved fat in a baking dish, then drain and add the chestnuts with salt and pepper. Stir to coat them with fat and roast them in the oven with the goose (after the heat has been lowered to 350° F) until they are glazed and very tender, 20 to 30 minutes.

5 For the mushrooms: Trim the stems of the mushrooms, discarding any dirt; wash them only if they are very sandy, draining them well. Melt a tablespoon of

the butter in a frying pan, add the mushrooms with salt and pepper, and cook, tightly covered, over very low heat until the juices run, 5 to 8 minutes. Remove the lid, raise the heat, and cook until the liquid evaporates, stirring occasionally. Cooking time varies from 5 to 10 minutes, depending on type and size.

6 Cream the remaining butter with the shallot, garlic, parsley, salt, and pepper and set it aside.

7 If you like your goose to be pink, test it after it has been roasting for a total of about 3 hours by pricking the thigh with a fork. The juices should run pink but not red, and the thigh should be slightly flexible when you wiggle it. If you prefer your goose well done, as we do, continue cooking until the juices from the leg run clear and the meat starts shrinking from the knuckle bone; the thigh will be almost loose.

8 When the goose is cooked, transfer it to a platter, cover it loosely with foil, and keep it warm. For the gravy, pour off the fat from the roasting pan, leaving behind the juices. Add the stock and simmer for 10 or 15 minutes, stirring to dissolve the pan juices. Strain the gravy into a small saucepan, taste it, and adjust the seasoning.

9 To finish: Reheat the chestnuts and mushrooms if necessary. Discard the trussing strings from the goose and pile the chestnuts around it on the platter. Stir the shallot butter into the mushrooms and pile them in a warm serving dish. Moisten the goose with a little gravy and serve the rest separately.

Chopped Liver
Lisa Schroeder
MOTHER'S BISTRO & BAR, PORTLAND, OREGON

Chef of the renowned Mother's Bistro in Portland, Oregon, Lisa Schroeder grew up in a household committed to food. In fact, her mother, Belle, was a chef who spent all day at her restaurant and then raced home to cook great meals for her family every night. In spite of her mother's passion for cooking, Lisa wasn't encouraged to learn to cook as a child. If she wasn't setting the table or doing dishes, Belle chased her out so she wouldn't be underfoot. But while Lisa undertook the more mundane kitchen duties, she watched her mother, soaking up as much as she could by osmosis. Still, cooking as a professional wasn't something she entertained as a real possibility until much later in life after the loss of her mother, a stint in marketing, and a failed marriage. It was during her unsatisfying thirteen-hour days in marketing and stops on the way home for Chinese take-out that Lisa began to yearn to be home, in the kitchen, cooking the meals that would nurture her daughter, just as her mother's meals had nurtured her. She longed to cook what she calls, "mother food" and began to think about a career in food for the first time in her life. A trip to the Culinary Institute of America crystallized her vision for a restaurant that would serve wholesome, home-style meals just like her mother used to make. Not even a stint at Le Cirque could dissuade her from following her dream to open a place called Mother's Bistro & Bar in 2000. The restaurant has become a tribute to mothers everywhere, featuring the food of a different mother every month. This Chopped Liver recipe is a nod to Lisa's Jewish roots and is a favorite, especially during the holidays.

MAKES 1 RING MOLD

3 tablespoons chicken fat
1 large onion, peeled and sliced
1 pound chicken livers
Salt and freshly ground black pepper
    to taste

5 eggs, hard-boiled and peeled, less one
    of the yolks (five egg whites and four
    egg yolks)
Matzo or water crackers, for serving

1 In a large sauté pan over high heat, melt the chicken fat.

2 Add the onion and continue to cook over high heat until the onion starts to brown. Lower the heat to medium and continue to cook until the onion is very soft and golden. Add the chicken livers and raise the heat to high.

3 Season the livers with salt and freshly ground black pepper and continue to cook until the livers are done (firm and cooked through).

4 Remove the pan from the heat and using a meat grinder or food processor, grind the livers along with the onion and eggs. If using a food processor, be careful not to process too much – the mixture should have a little texture; it should not be a paste. Once all of the mixture has been ground, mix with a wooden spoon. Taste the mixture and adjust the seasoning with salt and freshly ground black pepper.

5 Spoon the chopped liver into an 8-inch ring mold, pressing down to be sure the mixture is well compacted. Refrigerate, preferably overnight. To unmold, dip the ring mold in hot water for 45 seconds. Lift it out of the water and dry the sides of the mold. Place a plate on top and turn the mold upside down, gently tapping to loosen. If it does not unmold easily, run a knife around the edges and then place a plate on top again and repeat the unmolding process. Serve with matzo or water crackers shingled around the sides of the chopped liver.

⊰ KITCHEN MEMORIES ⊱

Living in Portland, Oregon, when I was about to open the restaurant, I was hell-bent on having my mother's chicken soup—you know, Jewish penicillin—and matzo balls, I mean, how could I not? In the back of my head I'm thinking, "Chopped liver, but who's going to want that?" Well I went to the only kosher deli in Portland and I tasted their chicken soup and was appalled, and then I tasted their chopped liver and I actually had to spit it out and I thought, "You know what, I owe it to the people of Portland to have good chopped liver."

Auntie Bheula's Oyster Stew
≋ *Gwen Kvavli Gulliksen* ≋

Of Norwegian descent, Gwen (pictured opposite) recalls eating things at home while growing up, such as rutabaga, turnips, and mushrooms, that were considered utterly exotic by her friends. Her family never ate processed foods; in fact, Gwen never even heard the term "from scratch" until she was in high school. And then she couldn't understand why anyone would cook any other way. Meals were extremely important to Gwen and her family—everyone was involved in planning dinners, and everyone always sat down and ate together, no matter what.

While Gwen was a graduate student pursuing degrees in Italian Renaissance Art and nineteenth-century France, she took a job at a wine boutique that had a small gourmet food section. The store owner was planning a vacation and wanted to leave Gwen in charge while he was gone. She asked if she could revamp the food section while he was out of town. When he came back he found that Gwen had filled half the store with food. A long trip to France followed, and Gwen was hooked. The art, the wine, and the food filled her life in a way that made perfect sense, and she put off starting her PhD to help a friend open a restaurant. From there, her career in food took off and has been punctuated by stints as Jean Louis Palladin's executive sous-chef at the Watergate Hotel as well the executive chef at the Getty Center. Today she is vice president of Pro*Act Specialties, procuring foods for wholesale produce companies around the country. Gwen continues to work as a chef, teacher, writer, and international food consultant, all while being a mom to her son Connor and preparing for the arrival of a new baby.

This recipe is one of her favorites—it's rich and delicious!

SERVES 4

1 clove garlic, mashed	2 cups milk
½ small onion, minced	1 can evaporated milk
½ stick unsalted butter, melted	Salt and pepper to taste
8 ounces oysters, liquid reserved, cut in half or quarters, depending on size	Oyster crackers

1 Sauté the garlic and onion in butter. Add the oysters and sauté until the edges curl.

2 Add the reserved oyster liquid, milk, and evaporated milk. Season with salt and pepper to taste. Heat but do not boil, as boiling will curdle the stew. Serve with oyster crackers.

⇥ KITCHEN MEMORIES ⇤

My aunts were really inspirational to me. My father's sister passed away very young of tuberculosis, so my mom's side of the family was our only family. Both sisters were excellent cooks. Aunt Bheula was very sophisticated. She lived in Chicago and was a good cook and would always pull out Chicken Diane from her freezer ready to go for dinner parties. She still does—I mean she's eighty-five years old and you'll go there and she'll have some delicious meal already made and pull it out of the freezer. She's a great entertainer, too. I have some of her recipes and try to use those for holidays, like Thanksgiving. Aunt Bheula did beautiful oyster stew. I try to make traditions of those things for my son, you know, by naming the recipes after my aunts so he'll have that history, too.

New Year's Tamales
Patricia Williams
MORRELLS RESTAURANT, NEW YORK

An accomplished ballerina with New York City's Opera Ballet, Patricia Williams exhibits an unusual combination of grace and backwoods survivalist who, since her retirement from dancing at age thirty, has established herself as one of America's great chefs. Her food has been described as having a Southwestern flair, which is no surprise considering the fact that she grew up in Texas surrounded by her mother's Mexican and Native American family. Before she could pirouette, she was out hunting and fishing with her brothers and her Welsh-Irish father and knew the finer points of dressing a deer. She was always surrounded by fresh food and wild game. In fact, to process everything they caught, her father built a "cook shack" where he made game and venison sausages in his smokehouse and grilled the spoils of the hunt on his built-in barbecues. The cook shack still stands, and Patricia's brothers have recently taken over the helm. Patricia had twelve aunts and uncles and about sixty cousins on her mother's side alone. Family gatherings included upwards of eighty family members who gathered around long banquet tables during holidays to assemble, cook, and serve traditional fare like these tamales.

SERVES 15

1¾ cups maseca (maseca, a tortilla corn flour masa mix, can be purchased at most grocery and specialty stores)
1 cup plus 2 tablespoons hot water
30 corn husks (or "shucks")

4 ounces vegetable shortening
3 tablespoons unsalted butter
1 teaspoon baking powder
1 cup chicken stock
Raisins as desired

1 Put the masa in the bowl of an electric mixer fitted with the paddle attachment. Slowly add the hot water and mix until it is all incorporated. Remove the mixture from the bowl of the mixer and allow to cool, completely, at room temperature.

2 Soak the corn husks in warm water for 2 hours.

3 In the bowl of the electric mixer, combine the vegetable shortening, butter, and baking powder and beat until fluffy. Add the cooled masa mixture to the butter in three stages, mixing well between additions.

4 Add ½ cup of chicken stock and mix thoroughly. After the first addition of chicken stock, test a small amount of the batter by dropping it in a glass of cold water. If it floats it will be tender when cooked. Add another ¼ cup of chicken stock and mix again. The mixture should be soft but not runny. Refrigerate for 1 hour.

Mom's Secret When making tamales of any kind, the corn husks, or "shucks" as some call them, have to be softened in warm water or they're impossible to fold properly. Shucks tend to float, making it hard to keep them wet.
To solve that problem, put a pan filled with water on top of the corn husks to keep them submerged. After the first hour of soaking, add more warm water to allow for the best absorption.

5 Remove the masa mixture from the refrigerator and add the remaining ¼ cup of chicken stock, taking care to incorporate it fully. If you would like to add raisins to the batter, now is the time to do so. For New Year's we would always put raisins in half the batter.

6 Begin heating water in a steamer for cooking the tamales.

7 Place two corn husks with the wide ends together. Using an ice cream scoop or a large spoon, place a mound of the masa mixture on the husks. Roll up and tie with torn strips of corn husk. Repeat until all the batter is used.

8 Place the tamales in the steamer, cover, and simmer over medium-low heat for 1½ hours. Throughout the cooking process, pay attention to the amount of water that remains in the steamer. If it runs out of water, the tamales will be tough.

⇥ KITCHEN MEMORIES ⇤

I was a ballet dancer until I was thirty, and then I retired. If you know anything about ballet dancers, you know they don't eat a lot. You're hungry and you want to eat all the time. It wasn't until I retired and went on my first big extended trip that I discovered the culinary world. I always wanted to live in France, so I took all my savings and moved to France for six months. It was twenty years ago and it was really just before the huge food movement began here in the United States. France had the beautiful fresh food and produce that I'd experienced growing up. Since it didn't matter if I gained weight, I was like a kid in a candy store, eating croissants, everything! As a woman traveling alone through Provence I got closer to the food because I was befriended by the owners of a lot of the mom-and-pop-type restaurants that I would frequent. When I ran out of money I came back to the United States and decided that cooking was what I wanted to do.

Cajun Shrimp
≈ Coleen Donnelly ≈

Like many of her colleagues, Coleen Donnelly didn't start out cooking. She discovered her passion for the culinary arts only after establishing herself as a computer programmer. About seven years into her high-tech career, she began giving dinner parties and realized how much she loved being in the kitchen, putting all her energy into a meal and having friends come over to enjoy it and exchange the stories of their day together. Cooking and computer programming had a lot in common, she discovered. Both require creativity and an inspired knack for seat-of-the-pants problem solving. The biggest difference was that in cooking, Coleen rediscovered a sense of home. Though she never cooked with her mother while growing up, she was always around while her mother was cooking, always sitting at the kitchen table doing homework or putting together a project (her grandmother and great-grandparents are pictured above). It's the warmth of those memories and moments that seem to have drawn her into the culinary world. Her first stop on the journey was the Culinary Institute of America where she "sucked every ounce of knowledge that [she] could out of the place and started off." She stopped first at New York City's famed Odeon Restaurant to take the helm as morning sous-chef before eventually heading off to open Magnolia, her own restaurant, where her mom's Cajun shrimp recipe figured prominently on the menu.

Mom's Secret If you don't live in a part of the country where fresh shrimp are readily available, it's best to buy them frozen. The majority of "fresh" grocery-store shrimp has been frozen and thawed, shortening its shelf life. Although it's tempting to buy deveined frozen shrimp to save time, don't do it—deveining and then freezing causes shrimp to lose flavor. Leaving the shells on during cooking in this recipe serves to intensify the flavors.

My mom used to make this fiery Cajun shrimp. We would all sit around the pot when it was ready and peel the shrimp. It is the sloppiest thing you could eat, and the most delicious thing, and it serves ten people, so she invited over however many people she needed and we'd all sit around the table and eat, talk, and drink wine. I wanted to put this on the menu at Magnolia, but I wanted it to work in the restaurant in a way that would make sense on the line, so I ended up rewriting the recipe using the same ingredients and creating a more high-end dish, but keeping it sort of low-country, serving it over grits, with a sauce that wasn't a broken sauce, so I reconfigured the whole thing.

SERVES 10 TO 12

5 pounds large shrimp
½ cup salt
Ice cubes
1 pound (4 sticks) unsalted butter
2 tablespoons minced garlic
1 teaspoon finely chopped fresh rosemary

4 tablespoons ground black pepper
½ cup Worcestershire sauce
2 teaspoons Tabasco
Juice of 2 lemons
2 teaspoons sea salt
2 whole lemons, sliced

1 Using a sharp paring knife, cut through the shell along the back of each shrimp all the way to the tail. Remove the vein that runs along the back, leaving the shell intact. Devein all 5 pounds in this manner.

2 Dissolve the ½ cup of salt in 1 gallon of cold water. Add the shrimp and ice cubes and let sit for 1 hour. This "brining" will enhance the flavor of the shrimp.

3 Preheat the oven to 400° F.

4 In a small saucepan, melt the butter. Add the garlic, rosemary, and pepper and cook briefly over low heat until the garlic has softened but not begun to color.

5 Add the Worcestershire sauce, Tabasco, lemon juice, and sea salt, and bring to a simmer. Remove from the heat.

6 In a casserole large enough to hold all of the shrimp, layer the shrimp, sauce, and lemon slices until all of the ingredients are used. Cover the casserole and bake for 15 to 20 minutes, or until the shrimp is cooked through. Serve immediately.

Kalsounakia
Ouzo Pastry filled with Ricotta Cheese
Fay Arouthianakis
Thom Thom, Wantagh, New York

Fay Arolithianakis (pictured with her family, opposite) is undeniably Greek and has a family that could have been lifted right off the silver screen—they even roast whole lambs on a spit in the backyard. When her parents immigrated to the United States from Greece, her father's first job here was as a dishwasher in a restaurant, and as Fay recalls, food has always played an integral role in their family life. Her mother cooks constantly and to this day will have a meal ready and waiting for Fay when she returns home late at night from the restaurant. In the Arolithianakis household, food is all about love and celebration, lessons deeply internalized by Fay as she moved from the Culinary Institute of America to a stint at the famed Rainbow Room, another at the Continental Club, and now, finally, a steak-and-sushi restaurant. Kalsounakia is a traditional food for special occasions on the island of Crete, and the recipe has been passed down for generations. Fay recommends serving it with a little ouzo or raki.

MAKES 25 TO 30 PASTRIES

DOUGH
3 cups all-purpose flour
1 teaspoon salt
2 ounces ouzo
Warm water as needed

FILLING
1 pound ricotta cheese
1 egg
Salt and pepper as needed
1 tablespoon chopped fresh mint

EGG WASH
2 eggs
2 tablespoons milk or cream

Olive oil for frying
Honey for garnish
Confectioners' sugar for garnish

1 For the dough: In an electric mixer fitted with the hook attachment, mix the flour, salt, and ouzo. When the ingredients are well mixed, begin adding small amounts of warm water until the dough becomes a firm ball, like pasta dough. Remove the dough from the mixing bowl, wrap in plastic, and let rest in the refrigerator for about 30 minutes.

2 While the dough is resting, combine the ricotta, egg, salt, pepper, and mint and mix well. Refrigerate.

3 After the dough has cooled for 30 minutes, begin rolling it through a hand-cranked pasta machine, stepping the rollers down one number at a time until the dough goes easily through the number-2 setting. (Note: The dough can be hand rolled as well, it is just less time-consuming to do it with a pasta machine.)

4 Leave the sheets as wide as the machine. Remove the ricotta mixture from the refrigerator and use a large spoon to scoop the cheese out onto the dough, leaving about an inch of dough between scoops. In a small bowl whisk together eggs and milk or cream to make the egg wash. Using a pastry brush, coat the edges of the dough as well as the spaces between the cheese scoops with the egg wash. Fold the other half of the dough over lengthwise (or cover it with a piece of similar length) and cut the dough between lumps of cheese, crimping the edges of each pastry with a fork as you work.

5 Pan-fry the pastries in olive oil until golden brown in color. The kalsounakia can be eaten plain or served drizzled with honey or sprinkled with sugar.

⚜ KITCHEN MEMORIES ⚜

Every time I go to Greece, everybody breaks out all the good dishes, and they kill three or four sheep for us to eat while we're there. My uncle still herds sheep. When somebody gets married or has a baby, everybody starts cooking. My aunt and grandmother still make cheese from the goat's milk, and one that's like a farmers cheese. My great-aunt showed my mom how to make this pastry dough from flour and ouzo that's filled with cheese and fried. When my dad was in Greece he brought back some cheese and we made it here. The dough used to be rolled with a long dowel. But now my aunt, the last time my mother was in Greece, showed her how to use the pasta machine, so it's less labor intensive and still it's as great as it was when I was a little kid.

Crab Buon Natale
～ *Cat Cora* ～
POSTINO, LAFAYETTE, CALIFORNIA

Cat Cora (pictured below) started her culinary career around age 8 by selling her Easy Bake Oven cakes to all the kids in her neighborhood. She wrote her first restaurant business plan when she was fifteen years old. She presented it to her god-father, Taki, a restaurateur in Jackson, Mississippi. Taki was a great inspiration to her, and, in the back of her mind, she always knew she wanted to be in the restaurant business. She started waiting tables to get experience. She'd be in the kitchen talking to the chefs, asking what herbs they were using, writing things down, and everyone would be yelling at her to get back out on the floor and take care of her tables! After work she'd go home and cook the things she'd seen in the restaurant. Her mother was impressed enough to let her go to culinary school, but Cat had her sights set on Europe because she thought she'd learn better at the "school of hard knocks."

By chance, right around the time Cat's mother mentioned culinary school, Julia Child, Marion Cunningham, and Robert Mondavi were doing book signings in Natchez, Mississippi, not far from Cat's home in Jackson. In that very intimate set-ting she was able to spend some time talking with all three culinary "legends" about their thoughts on culinary schools and the restaurant business in general. Julia Child gave her opinion and Marion Cunningham gave Cat her home phone number

and told her to call if she needed anything after a forty-five minutes conversation. Cat was blown away. Her passion was ignited and she immediately began looking into Julia's top pick, the Culinary Institute of America, to which she was quickly accepted.

A later move to the Napa Valley led Cat to Lafayette, California, where, in an old post office build-ing, she opened a new restaurant, aptly named Postino. Cat was the executive chef for several years before breaking away to pursue other interests, including a starring role in Melting Pot, a Food Network produc-tion. She recently published *Cat Cora's Kitchen*.

Growing up Greek in the American South,

Cat Cora's formative years were filled with great food. Fresh goat cheese and home-cured olives arrived regularly from relatives still living in Greece on the island of Skopelos, and southern spices enhanced even traditional Greek meals. In her mother's kitchen she'd sit up on the counter or stand on a step stool stirring nothing in a bowl proudly, exclaiming, "Momma, I's cookin', I's cookin'!" Cat still she loves cooking at home. One of her favorite recipes for the holidays is Crab Buon Natale, with an underlying nod to both her Mediterranean and southern heritages.

SERVES 4

4 (1- to 1½-pound) Dungeness crabs, cooked, cleaned, and cracked (reserve juices and tomalley)
1 teaspoon chile flakes
1 tablespoon chopped fresh thyme
10 cloves garlic, minced
5 tablespoons fresh lemon juice
1 cup mayonnaise
½ cup (1 stick) butter
4 tablespoons extra virgin olive oil

2 tablespoons lemon zest
1½ teaspoons kosher salt
1 teaspoon freshly cracked black pepper
3 tablespoons roughly chopped flat-leaf parsley
Lemon wedges for garnish
4 slices rustic bread, toasted, rubbbed with garlic cloves, and drizzled with olive oil

1 Preheat the oven to 500°F.

2 Push the crab tomalley through a sieve into a small saucepan. Add the chile flakes, 1 teaspoon of the thyme, just under one-half of the minced garlic, and 1 tablespoon of the lemon juice. Add in the reserved crab juice, mix, and bring to a simmer. Stir quickly and remove from the heat. Pour into a small mixing bowl and allow the sauce to cool.

3 Once the sauce has cooled, add the mayonnaise and check the seasoning. Adjust as needed. Set aside.

4 In a large sauté pan, heat the butter, olive oil, the remaining minced garlic, and the lemon zest over medium-high heat until hot. Add the crab, season with salt, pepper, and remaining thyme, and mix well. Place the pan in the oven and bake until the crab is hot throughout and the garlic is golden brown. Drizzle with 4 tablespoons of lemon juice and scatter the parsley over the top.

5 To serve, stack the crab on a platter and drizzle the mayonnaise all over (it can also be served on the side). Place the lemons and the rustic toast around and serve warm.

Baked Alaska
⇜ Emily Luchetti ⇝
FARALLON, SAN FRANCISCO

Growing up in Corning, New York, in the 1960s might have been a complete disaster for the developing taste buds of pastry chef Emily Luchetti had it not been for parents with a penchant for playing with food. Subscribers to *Gourmet* magazine since their marriage in 1952, the Luchettis were the typical American family except that they enjoyed experimenting in the kitchen. Emily's dad would save margarine tubs all year, and then at Christmastime he'd use them as pâté molds. Today the irony of those margarine/pâté tubs isn't lost on Emily, but back then the flavors and textures her parents introduced were thrilling and opened the door to a world that the frozen vegetables of her western New York State home might never have allowed her to explore. She remembers how her family ate together at the table every night. Beef fondue was common. Once, when she asked her mom why they ate it so often, her mom said it was so that the family would stay longer at the table, both cooking and eating together.

Right after Emily started college, her parents moved to Sanibel Island, Florida, where they opened a cookware shop. Emily worked there during the summers and loved it. Emily's parents supported her decision to attend the New York Restaurant School, where she made the decision to pursue cooking as a full-time profession.

Her first job as a pastry chef was at Stars Restaurant in San Francisco, where she remained for ten years before moving on to open Farallon with Chef Mark Franz in 1997. This Baked Alaska recipe is a favorite and frequent Christmas dessert request by her nieces and nephew (pictured opposite with Emily).

Mom's Secret Don't have a pastry bag and tips lying around the house? Most home cooks are more likely to have Ziploc bags in their kitchen drawer than they are a pastry bag. Fill a Ziploc bag with meringue, squeeze it down into one corner, cut off a small piece of the corner, and use the bag to pipe meringue onto the ice cream. You won't get the pattern or control of a pastry bag fitted with a star tip, but in a pinch, this method works really well.

⅔ cup hazelnuts, toasted and skinned

2 cups all-purpose flour

2 cups firmly packed dark brown sugar

2 teaspoons baking soda

1 teaspoon baking powder

2 large eggs

8 tablespoons (1 stick) unsalted butter, melted and cooled

1 cup buttermilk

1 cup freshly squeezed orange juice

8 scoops chocolate ice cream (your favorite brand)

1 cup (about 8 large) egg whites

2 cups granulated sugar

2½ teaspoons instant espresso

1   Preheat the oven to 350° F. Grease and flour a 11 x 16-inch baking pan with 1-inch sides. Finely grind the hazelnuts with the flour in a food processor. Transfer the mixture to a bowl and add the brown sugar, baking soda, and baking powder.

2   In a small bowl, whisk together the eggs and melted butter. Stir the egg mixture into the dry ingredients. Stir in the buttermilk and the orange juice. Spread the batter into the prepared pans. Bake until a skewer inserted in the middle comes out clean, about 25 minutes. Cool to room temperature.

3   Cut the cake into 8 (3½-inch) circles. Place the cake circles several inches apart on a baking tray. Place a scoop of chocolate ice cream on top of each cake circle. Place the tray in the freezer.

4   Preheat the oven to 450° F. Combine the egg whites and the granulated sugar in the top of a double boiler. Lightly whisk the mixture over medium heat (so the water is at a simmer) until the egg mixture is hot. Transfer the egg whites to the bowl of an electric mixer and whip on medium-high speed until the egg whites are thick and cool. Fold in the instant espresso. Place the egg whites in a pastry bag fitted with a ½-inch star tip. Pipe the egg whites over the chocolate ice cream, completely covering it but leaving the cake exposed. Freeze the baked Alaskas for 1 hour. Bake until the meringue is golden brown, about 5 minutes. Transfer to plates with a metal spatula. Serve immediately.

The Sanders's Christmas Bread
❧ *Barbara Sanders* ❧

The early part of Barbara Sanders's (pictured with her granddaughter, opposite) childhood was spent on a dairy farm in Lyme, New Hampshire. There was always an abundance of eggs, butter, milk, cream, and chickens, but Barbara doesn't think she even knew what a steak was until she was a teenager. Her parents divorced when she was two and remarried about eight years later, which was around the time her grandfather sold the family farm and moved into town. Rather than work in the copper mines in Vermont, which was about the only job her father could find at the time, he bought some old bakery equipment and set up a bakery in a one-car garage. He went door-to-door selling baked goods in a truck he fitted with shelves that were designed to keep a single pie from bouncing around as he drove through town. At that time, just after WWII had ended, people were still in the habit of making their own breads and pastries, so it was a hard sell. Eventually, though, her father became successful enough to open a bakery on Main Street in Hanover, New Hampshire.

Bread has always played a large role in Barbara's life, it seems. It even "bought" her daughter, Deborah, a horse in the 1970s. At that time people were accustomed to bartering for goods and services, and so Barbara and her daughter entered into an agreement with a local family whereby she and Deborah baked bread for this family once every two weeks for a year, at which point Deborah took ownership of the horse.

MAKES TWO 1/2-POUND BRAIDED LOAVES

1 package active dry yeast
⅓ cup warm water (110° F)
½ cup sugar
½ cup vegetable shortening
2 teaspoons salt
⅔ cup milk
5 to 5¼ cups all-purpose flour, sifted
3 eggs, lightly beaten, plus 2 additional
    beaten eggs for egg wash
2 teaspoons vegetable oil

DECORATION
Confectioners' sugar
Lemon juice
Red candied cherries
Green candied cherries
Chopped nuts

1 In a small bowl, soften the yeast in the warm water.

2 In a saucepan, combine the sugar, shortening, salt, and milk. Scald while stirring until the shortening melts and sugar dissolves. Cool to lukewarm.

3 Add 1½ cups of flour to the cooled milk mixture and beat well. Add the softened yeast and 3 beaten eggs. Beat well again. Stir in the remaining flour until a soft dough is formed. (You may not need all the flour.)

4 Turn the dough out onto a floured surface. Knead slightly until it is soft and elastic (5 to 8 minutes). Place the dough in a large bowl, lightly greased with the oil, turning once to coat the entire surface of the dough with oil. Cover the bowl and allow the dough to rise in a warm place until doubled in size (about 3 hours).

5 After the dough has doubled, punch it down and turn it out onto a lightly floured surface. Divide the dough into two equal pieces and then divide each of these into three equal pieces. Roll each piece into a 12- to 14-inch long piece. Place each piece side-by-side in two groups of three, press the ends of each group of three together, and braid the loaves, taking care to press the ends together at the end of the braid as well. Place the braids on parchment paper on a baking sheet and allow to rise in a warm place for about an hour until doubled in size again.

6 Preheat the oven to 350° F.

7 Brush both loaves with egg wash to give the finished loaves a deep rich-brown color, and bake for 20 to 30 minutes. Check under the braids for medium browning, which indicates the braids are properly baked. Remove from the oven and allow to cool completely before decorating.

8 Decorate according to your taste. You can make a paste by adding a few drops of lemon juice to confectioners' sugar and then spread on top of the bread. To be fancy, place a green cherry quarter on each side of a red cherry half to make a flower. Or you can just sprinkle nuts on top.

Maraschino Cherry Cake
❧ *Rachel Stewart* ❧

Rachel Stewart was, perhaps, the most precocious child of the chefs interviewed for this book. She cooked her first meal for her parents when she was four—chicken à la king in a bag, biscuits from a can, and Jell-O. At the age of five she orchestrated a surprise thirtieth birthday party for her mother. She called all the guests herself to announce the party and told them what to bring. Rachel, a midwesterner of German descent, grew up in Indiana, the only child of cattle farmers in a world filled with hamburgers, steaks, and a wide variety of Jell-O mold desserts. As an adult Rachel found her way into the corporate world, where she spent twenty years in the travel business working as a corporate trainer for American Express before she decided to make a move out into the culinary world in 1996 to found her company, Kitchen Magician. Today, she is widely recognized as one of the most innovative personal chefs in the San Francisco Bay area.

ONE 8-INCH TWO-LAYER CAKE

2¼ cups cake flour
3 teaspoons baking powder
½ teaspoon salt
1⅓ cups sugar
½ cup vegetable shortening
¼ cup maraschino cherry juice

16 maraschino cherries, cut into eight
   pieces each
½ cup milk
½ to ⅔ cup unbeaten egg whites
½ cup chopped nuts, any variety
Snowball Frosting (recipe follows)

1 Preheat the oven to 350° F. Grease and flour two 8-inch round cake pans.

2 In a large bowl, sift together the cake flour, baking powder, salt, and sugar.

3 In another bowl, combine the shortening, cherry juice, cherries, and milk. Beat for 2 minutes, then add to the sifted flour mixture. Mix to combine, then add the unbeaten egg whites and beat for 2 more minutes. Fold in the nuts.

4 Pour the batter into the prepared baking pans and bake for 30 to 35 minutes or until toothpick comes out clean. Cool in pans for several minutes, then unmold onto wire racks. Cool completely before frosting.

5 Place one layer on serving plate and spread with approximately ¾ cup of frosting, then frost top and sides with remaining frosting.

SNOWBALL FROSTING

MAKES ABOUT 3 CUPS (ENOUGH TO FROST TWO 9-INCH LAYERS)

2¼ cups granulated sugar
½ cup water (or maraschino cherry juice
   if you prefer a pink frosting)
3 tablespoons corn syrup

3 egg whites, stiffly beaten
3 tablespoons powdered sugar
1 tablespoon vanilla extract

1 Combine the sugar, water or cherry juice, and corn syrup in a small saucepan over medium-high heat. Boil until it reaches the soft ball stage (238° F on a candy thermometer).

2 Add the syrup in a fine stream to the beaten egg whites, beating to incorporate.

3 While continuing to beat, add powdered sugar and vanilla until stiff peaks form and frosting is cool to the touch. You can make this in advance and store it in the refrigerator for up to a day. If it's too stiff to spread, add a few drops of boiling water and mix to soften.

⇥ KITCHEN MEMORIES ⇤

When I left a good corporate job, my mother became my silent partner because we all know that the food business is not a real good place from which to pay the rent. And she trusted me enough that she paid for my medical insurance and long term-disability. She would periodically say, "Here's a gift for my partner because I know that you are doing what you love and there's nothing that I could hope for more than to see my only child doing something that makes her happy." I'm really blessed by that. I know a lot of people don't have that relationship or that opportunity, and I miss her so much.

Gâteau Rolla
❧ *Joyce Goldstein* ❧

In Joyce Goldstein's childhood home "everything was cooked to a certain death. Vegetables were gray, lamb stew was greasy with gray peas—it was horrible," she says. What saved her palate from a certain death was eating out in restaurants, which she did twice a week with her family as she was growing up. It's hard to believe that America's quintessential Jewish mother and author of nineteen cookbooks didn't do much cooking until she was in graduate school, at which point she started teaching herself to cook with a 1952 copy of *The Joy of Cooking, The New York Times Cookbook,* and the works of Elizabeth David and Paula Peck. After graduate school, in 1959, she and her husband went to Italy on a Fulbright for a year. It was in Italy that she began the "longest love affair of her life," broadening her knowledge base about food as she made daily trips to the local markets, where she chatted with butchers and dairy and produce vendors about how they used their products. She'd have a meal and rush home to cook what she'd just eaten so she could remember what it tasted like.

After she and her husband returned to the United States in 1960, they had three children in quick succession, and Joyce's aspirations to pursue art came to an abrupt halt. She turned, once again, to the kitchen as a creative outlet and began cooking her way through the *Time/Life Foods of the World* series. In 1965 she began teaching and "never looked back." A stint at the famed Chez Panisse, the opening of her own restaurant Square One, and all those cookbooks later, Joyce continues to pursue a variety of food-related projects, including a cookbook pairing recipes with wines, along with her sommelier son, Evan. This Gâteau Rolla recipe is her grandchildren's favorite birthday cake.

MAKES 1 (9-INCH) LAYER CAKE

MERINGUES
6 egg whites
Pinch salt
1 cup sugar
1 teaspoon vanilla extract
1 cup ground blanched almonds

FROSTING
6 ounces semisweet chocolate
2 tablespoons unsweetened cocoa
3 egg whites
¾ cup sugar
1½ cups (3 sticks) unsalted butter, softened

1 Preheat the oven to 250° F. Oil two large flat baking sheets with no raised sides to make it easier to slip off the finished meringues. Trace a 9-inch circle onto 4 (10- to 11-inch) squares of baker's parchment paper. Place the paper squares on the baking sheets, pencil sides down. Oil the paper lightly.

2 Beat the egg whites with a pinch of salt until stiff. Gradually beat in ¾ cup of the sugar. Beat the meringue until stiff and glossy. On low speed, beat in the vanilla and the remaining ¼ cup of sugar. Fold in the almonds. Spread or pipe (with a pastry bag) this mixture onto the parchment, staying within the guidelines of the circles. Do not make these meringues too thick or they will not dry out easily. About ¼ inch is ideal. Bake the meringues for about 1 hour. They will be dry and firm, but not brown. Carefully remove to a rack to cool. Peel off the paper. If one should break or crack, it can be patched with frosting.

3 Melt the chocolate and cocoa in the top of a double boiler and set aside. Beat the egg whites, over a bowl or double boiler of hot water, until they are foamy and hot to the touch. Gradually beat in the ¾ cup of sugar, then the softened butter, a bit at a time, then the melted chocolate. Beat the frosting until smooth. Chill until firm enough to spread.

4 Assemble the cake by spreading layers of chocolate frosting between the layers of meringue. Then cover the top and sides with the rest of the frosting. Refrigerate overnight. Bring to room temperature before serving. Slice with a serrated knife.

⊰ KITCHEN MEMORIES ⊱

I have two grandchildren. Adam is seven and Elena is ten. Both are Evan's kids, and they have both assisted me in the kitchen, but my grandson is really the one who is interested in cooking and baking. He has his own cookbook and measuring cups, and he can read recipes, and he has opinions. Even when he was two or three he could taste something and say for example, "There's ginger in this." He has announced to me, "Grandma, I think I have the Goldstein mouth!" My granddaughter also has very definite opinions about food. Gâteau Rolla is a recipe that I got from one of the early *Gourmet* magazines. They tell you to put the meringue on wax paper, and the meringue melts into the paper, and it's really an epic struggle to get the meringue off the paper. The first few times I made the cake, I swore I'd never make it again. Then I discovered parchment paper and it was a piece of cake. The grandchildren always tease me about the waxed paper.

Chapter Six
Indulgences

DESSERT IS A FAVORITE PART OF ANY MEAL. Moreover, judging by the number of dessert recipes contributed for this book, sweet dishes seem to best embody the comforts of hearth and home. Of course, we women have always known that! It's easier to soothe a broken heart with a warm plate of chocolate chip cookies and a cold glass of milk than a strip steak any day. Moms always seem to know that a chocolate dessert can make even the worst day at school seem like a distant memory. And there's nothing more refreshing than a slice of lemon pie when you're down in the dumps!

We've included a wide variety of recipes in this chapter, from Emily Luchetti's simple, yet delicious, Chocolate Chip Cookies to Sherry Yard's more complex but equally soothing Banana–Chocolate Chip Soufflé. There are some recipes, like Coleen Donnelly's Orange Slice Cookies, that will give even the most seasoned sweet eaters something new to try.

Brooklyn Baci
～ *Sherry Yard* ～
SPAGO, LOS ANGELES

If Sherry Yard, currently pastry chef at Spago, learned anything at all from her mother, it was how *not* to cook. After talking with nearly one hundred chefs for this book, all of whom had in some way been inspired by their mothers to cook and bring people together for a meal, we couldn't believe that Sherry had developed any passion for cooking at all! Our favorite story was of the time Sherry's mother, Ann, who had a habit of heating cans of vegetables by placing the cans, without their lids, directly in the oven, forgot to remove the lids. The cans heated up and before long, the oven door burst open and a can of creamed corn flew out, whizzing past Sherry's crudité-making grandmother's head and coming to a stop as it hit a plate glass door across the room. If nothing else, cooking was exciting at Sherry's house!

Fortunately, her grandmother Ann Cartwright-Jest, or "Hooter," as she was nicknamed, lived just around the corner from Sherry's childhood Brooklyn home and was Sherry's greatest early culinary inspiration. These "baci," which means "give me many kisses" in Italian, reminds Sherry of Hooter.

MAKES 4 DOZEN COOKIES

1 ½ cups all-purpose flour

½ cup unsweetened cocoa powder

2 ounces bittersweet chocolate, finely chopped

6 ounces (1 ½ sticks) cold unsalted butter, cut into ½-inch pieces

½ cup granulated sugar

2 tablespoons honey

1 teaspoon instant espresso powder

1 teaspoon vanilla extract

¼ teaspoon salt

1 large egg, at room temperature

2 tablespoons heavy cream

1 cup confectioners' sugar, sifted

1 Preheat the oven to 350° F. Adjust the rack to the lower third of the oven. Line two baking sheets with parchment paper.

2 Sift the flour and cocoa powder into a medium bowl and set aside.

3 Fill a small saucepan three-quarters full of water and bring to a simmer over medium heat. Place the chocolate in a small bowl and place it over the simmering water, creating a double boiler. Stir occasionally until the chocolate is melted,

about 5 minutes. Remove the bowl from the heat and set aside.

4 Using a standing mixer fitted with a paddle attachment or a hand mixer, cream the butter on medium speed until pale yellow, about 2 minutes. Scrape down the sides of the bowl and the paddle. Add the sugar, honey, instant espresso powder, vanilla, and salt. Cream on medium speed until smooth and lump-free, about 1 minute. Stop the mixer and scrape down the sides of the bowl and the paddle.

5 Add the chocolate and beat on medium speed for 30 seconds. Add the egg and beat until fully incorporated, about 15 seconds.

6 On low speed, add the flour mixture. Beat until all the dry ingredients are incorporated. Scrape down the sides of the bowl. Add the cream and mix it in, about 30 seconds.

Mom's Secret If you plan on freezing these cookies after they are baked, underbake them slightly, thaw, and crisp the cookies in a 350° F oven for 5 minutes before serving.

7 Transfer the dough to a large piping bag fitted with a medium (#4) plain tip. Pipe the dough onto the prepared baking sheet in kiss shapes. To achieve a kiss, touch the pastry tip to the tray and squeeze the bag, pulling straight up as you squeeze. Stop squeezing when the cookie is 1 inch in diameter and quickly lift the bag straight up. Sift confectioners' sugar over the kisses.

8 Bake one sheet at a time for 12 to 15 minutes, or until firm and dry to the touch, turning the sheet front to back halfway through the baking. Cool on a rack before serving. You can store these in an airtight container for 3 days at room temperature. The cookies can also be frozen for up to 1 month.

Banana–Chocolate Chip Soufflé
❧ Sherry Yard ❧
SPAGO, LOS ANGELES
MAKES 8 INDIVIDUAL SOUFFLÉS

BANANA SCHMUTZ

1 tablespoon unsalted butter

¼ cup granulated sugar

¼ cup packed light brown sugar

1½ large, very ripe bananas, peeled and
   cut into ½-inch pieces

⅛ cup dark rum

1½ teaspoons fresh lemon juice

Pinch salt (less than half of ⅛ teaspoon)

CHOCOLATE SAUCE

¼ cup granulated sugar

2 ounces unsweetened chocolate

6 ounces bittersweet chocolate

¼ cup heavy cream

¼ cup crème fraîche

2 tablespoons unsalted butter

2 tablespoons Tia Maria

SOUFFLÉS

2 tablespoons unsalted butter, melted

¼ cup sugar for the ramekins, plus
   ½ cup

1 cup Banana Schmutz (above),
   at room temperature

½ cup finely chopped bittersweet
   chocolate

8 large egg whites

Pinch of cream of tartar (less than
   ⅛ teaspoon)

FOR THE BANANA SCHMUTZ

1   In a large sauté pan, melt the butter over medium heat until the solids separate, sink to the bottom, and begin to brown, 3 to 5 minutes. When the butter is a dark golden color, add the sugar and brown sugar and stir until dissolved, 5 to 8 minutes.

2   Add the bananas and sauté, stirring constantly, for about 2 minutes, or until the bananas are softened and caramelized. Remove from the heat and carefully add the rum, lemon juice, and salt. Place the pan back over low heat and cook for 1 minute more.

3   Remove from the heat and immediately spoon half of the banana mixture into a food processor. (Be careful: the mixture is molten!) Pulse until the mixture becomes a smooth paste. Remove and repeat with the remaining banana mixture. Use the warm schmutz immediately or cool and refrigerate in an airtight container for up to 3 days.

FOR THE CHOCOLATE SAUCE:

1 Make a simple syrup by combining the sugar and ¼ cup of water in a small saucepan over high heat. Stir to moisten the sugar and insert a candy thermometer. Cook until the temperature reaches 220° F, about 5 minutes. Immediately remove from the heat and allow to cool. Measure out ¼ cup; discard the rest.

2 Using a serrated knife, finely chop the chocolates into ¼ -inch pieces and place in a medium heatproof bowl.

3 Bring the cream, crème fraîche, and butter to a boil in a small saucepan over medium heat. Immediately pour the cream over the chopped chocolate. Tap the bowl on the counter to settle the chocolate into the cream, then let it sit for 1 minute. Using a rubber spatula, slowly stir in a circular motion, starting from the center of the bowl and working out to the sides. Stir until all the chocolate is melted, about 2 minutes.

4 Add the Tia Maria and simple syrup and stir for 1 minute, or until smooth and thoroughly combined. Cover the sauce and keep it warm near the stove until it is served.

FOR THE SOUFFLÉS:

1 Preheat the oven to 375° F. Lightly coat eight 6- to 8-ounce ramekins with melted butter and then lightly but completely dust them with sugar and place on a baking sheet. Combine the banana schmutz and chopped chocolate pieces in a medium bowl and set aside at room temperature.

2 Using a standing mixture fitted with the whisk attachment or a hand mixer, whip the egg whites for about 30 seconds, or until soft foam appears. Add the cream of tartar and as the whites are whipping, slowly sprinkle in the sugar. Whip the whites for 1 to 2 minutes more, or until they reach the medium-peak stage.

3 Using a rubber spatula, fold one-third of the egg whites into the banana mixture. Carefully fold in the remaining whites to avoid deflating the mixture.

4 Spoon the soufflé into the prepared ramekins, filling them to the rim. Smooth the tops with a metal spatula. Gently run a paring knife around the inside edge of each ramekin. This creates a wall of air that helps the soufflé rise up straight. Place the ramekins on a baking sheet.

5 Bake for 15 to 20 minutes, or until tall, golden brown, dry on the edges, and creamy in the center. Serve immediately with chocolate sauce.

Blueberry Clafouti
Stephanie Kimmel
MARCHÉ, EUGENE, OREGON

The daughter of an airforce pilot, Stephanie Kimmel grew up all over the world. From Japan to Libya and Germany, Stephanie's Texan family followed her father wherever his job took them. There was, as Stephanie said, no cozy, unchanging home kitchen that influenced her culinary development. Instead, she was fortunate to be exposed to global cuisines and cultures at a very young age. She has always loved to eat and because of her early exposure to such a wide range of foods and flavors, she began dabbling in the kitchen when she was quite young. She was in graduate school getting a doctorate in comparative literature before she abandoned her academic career in favor of the restaurant business.

Along the way she was married and had a daughter, Leah, with whom she stayed at home, earning money as a freelance editor and writer for a time before her longing for the restaurant business inspired her to open her own place. She and her husband opened the Excelsior Café, with eight tables and innovative Northwest cuisine, in April 1972. Stephanie opened a new restaurant with a toddler and a baby on the way and cooked right up to the day Katya was born. Both daughters literally grew up in the business. Her latest venture is Marché restaurant, where she works with both her daughter Leah and her son-in-law Rocky.

This clafouti recipe is a perfect dessert to take along on a picnic and is especially good served with whipped cream or ice cream.

SERVES 5 GENEROUSLY

1 pint blueberries

1 cup sifted unbleached flour

¼ teaspoon salt

2 cups milk

3 extra large eggs

½ cup sugar

1 teaspoon vanilla extract

Unsalted butter for dotting the top

Confectioners' sugar, for garnish

Whipped cream, for garnish (optional)

Kirsch, for garnish

1 Preheat the oven to 425° F. Butter and flour a 10-inch porcelain tart dish or other attractive ovenproof, nonreactive dish. Distribute the blueberries evenly over the bottom of the dish. Place the dish on a rimmed cookie sheet.

Mom's Secret Clafouti is an ancient French country dessert that uses whatever fresh fruit is in season. Its origins are in the Limousin region of central France, where it originally was made with black cherries. Stephanie likes to use McKenzie River Valley blueberries. Highly adaptable and always appreciated, the simple sweet batter is a breeze to make. She recommends serving the clafouti when it is still a bit warm, but notes that it is also delicious at room temperature.

2 In a large mixing bowl, combine the flour and salt, then add 1 cup of the milk and whisk well to combine. Add the eggs, one at a time, until they are incorporated. Whisk in the sugar, the vanilla, and the remaining cup of milk. Ladle the batter over the berries in the dish, then dot the top with small bits of cold unsalted butter.

3 Place the clafouti on a rack in the middle of the oven, being careful not to spill any batter over the rim of the pan. Bake until puffed and golden brown, about 35 minutes. Allow to cool enough to set. Garnish with a generous dusting of confectioners' sugar, or even a dollop of whipped cream scented with a few drops of kirsch if you're feeling extravagant.

⊰ KITCHEN MEMORIES ⊱

My grandparents on both sides were farmers and my dad's side of the family was in west Texas. They raised livestock of all kinds—sheep, cattle, lots of hogs, chickens. My grandmother had a wonderful garden, and they had dairy cows. They'd go into town on Saturdays to buy coffee, Dr. Pepper, sugar, things like that, but otherwise they were remarkably self-sufficient. They had a smokehouse and pumped water. I loved staying there. I adored my grandmother, and she was the one who got me excited about cooking. One of my first memories of cooking with her is the time we made peach ice cream. The peaches came from the tree in her yard, and we collected the eggs and skimmed the cream off the top of the milk. I can still taste that today. We even had to heat the water on the stove to wash dishes. I'm so happy I had a chance to experience life like that—that kind of simple and pure family farm lifestyle is pretty much gone nowadays.

Ruth's Pineapple Upside-Down Cake
Mary Sue Milliken
BORDER GRILL, SANTA MONICA AND LAS VEGAS
CIUDAD, LOS ANGELES

As much as she enjoyed cooking and her home economics classes in high school, Mary Sue Milliken couldn't have guessed that she'd become a celebrity chef as she pedaled to her first job at a doughnut shop on a green banana-seat Sting Ray at age fourteen. She fibbed about her age to get the job, where she filled and dipped doughnuts at 4:00 A.M. before changing into a little pink dress and serving coffee and doughnuts to commuters at 5:30 A.M. five days a week before school started. During a trip to Chicago to visit her sister at Northwestern University, Mary Sue was a guest at a dinner party where she discovered her interest in cooking as a profession. One of the hosts, a professionally trained chef, told her that he could help get her into Washburn Trade School for culinary arts. She decided then and there that's what she was going to do and returned to high school with a sense of purpose that enabled her to graduate a year early.

A two-year waiting list prevented Mary Sue from entering Washburn Trade School immediately following graduation, but she moved to Chicago anyway and her sister's friend got the wait reduced to nine months. She's been working in professional kitchens ever since, starting with the Conrad Hilton Hotel, with moves to Maxim's and Le Perroquet, where she met her business partner, Susan Feniger.

Mary Sue's mother (pictured below with Mary Sue) was her primary culinary influence. She was always very interested in food—in fact, to this day, Mary Sue says

that her mother's e-mails to her "detail everything she ate every minute of the day."

Mary Sue's mom worked with Mary Sue and Susan Feniger at City Café and during her time there made everything from Pineapple Upside-Down Cake to pâté. This cake caused a kitchen fight between the chef and her mother (see Kitchen Memories, below). As you can see here, Mary Sue won the fight and the cake is made with fresh pineapple!

⊰ KITCHEN MEMORIES ⊱

During my childhood my mom was a really, really grumpy single mom with three kids. She worked her butt off, and she wasn't doing anything she was really very passionate about—teaching school, selling real estate. Years later, after I'd been out here in Vegas for a few years, I said, "I'm so sick of listening to you complain about your job, come out here and work for us—we'll give you a job in the pastries." I taught her all my recipes and she was a real asset in the kitchen; she made yogurt, sauerkraut, sausages, and pâtés. We did have one big fight though. I wanted pineapple upside-down cake and she said it was a waste of time to make it using fresh pineapple. She didn't want to cut all the fresh pineapple, so she made side-by-side comparison cakes, even cutting the fresh pineapple to look exactly like the canned pineapple, I could still tell which was which. She was so mad because we asked her to continue to make it with fresh pineapple!

SERVES 8 TO 12

14 tablespoons (1¾ sticks) unsalted butter
¾ cup light brown sugar
½ medium fresh pineapple, peeled, cored, and cut into ½-inch slices
1 cup granulated sugar
2 eggs, at room temperature
¼ cup dark rum
2 cups cake flour
1½ teaspoons baking powder
¾ teaspoon baking soda
½ teaspoon salt
½ cup buttermilk

1 Preheat the oven to 375° F. In a 10-inch cast-iron skillet or a 10-inch cake pan, melt 6 tablespoons of the butter and add the brown sugar, stirring over low heat to incorporate. Remove from the heat and arrange the pineapple slices to cover the bottom of the pan.

2 Cream the remaining 1 stick butter and the sugar in an electric mixer fitted with a paddle. Add one egg at a time and the dark rum until incorporated, scraping the sides occasionally. In a separate bowl, sift the flour, baking powder, baking soda, and salt. While the mixer is running slowly, add the flour mixture and buttermilk alternating (ending with buttermilk). Pour into the cake pan or skillet that has been prelined with the brown sugar–butter mixture and the slices of fresh pineapple.

3 Bake for 35 to 45 minutes, or until a toothpick inserted in the center comes out clean. Cool and flip onto a serving plate.

Bertha Hall's Chess Pie

Katy Keck

THE NEW WORLD GRILL, NEW YORK

This pie has always been special to Katy (see the box below). As an eight-year-old she recorded the recipe on an index card with little notes to herself, like "When you set the oven back to 350 degrees, keep the pie in the oven. Don't take it out." Recently she discovered, through a local newspaper article, that this pie was actually passed down from her great-grandmother, Mrs. Robert Highman. Katy loves the fact that the pie comes from her great-grandmother because she has her wedding china, which dates to the 1880s. Katy thinks it's fitting to serve the pie on her china.

MAKES ONE 9-INCH PIE

CRUST

1½ cups all-purpose flour

½ teaspoon salt

½ cup vegetable shortening

¼ cup cold water

FILLING

½ cup unsalted butter or margarine

1½ cups granulated sugar

3 eggs

1 teaspoon white vinegar

1 teaspoon cornmeal

1 teaspoon vanilla extract

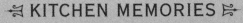

⊰ KITCHEN MEMORIES ⊱

Grandmother Keck made the best crust. She handled everything so delicately—
she always said for biscuits and pie crusts, "Touch it like you're handling hot
coals." She was such a sturdy cook, but she also had a very light touch when it
came to things like baking. One of the pies that was very traditional in our family was chess pie. It's basically just a sugar pie! But I love it. I remember running
home when I was probably seven or eight years old, having just baked a chess
pie with Grandmother Keck. Grandmother Keck wasn't one of those people who
had to teach or lecture. She just thought you should get right in and assumed
you'd get it. She gave me a lot of courage and inspiration to try new things.

1 Preheat the oven to 350° F.

2 For the crust: In a medium-sized mixing bowl, sift together the flour and salt.
Using two forks or a pastry blender, mix the flour, salt, and vegetable shortening
until the shortening is reduced to pea-sized pieces.

3 Add the cold water and blend until the mixture begins to form a ball. Knead
the dough lightly and refrigerate for at least 30 minutes.

4 Remove the dough from the refrigerator and roll into a sheet large enough to
fill a 9-inch pie pan. Trim and crimp the edges of the dough. Before baking, dock,
or poke holes in, the dough on the bottom of the pan to prevent it from bubbling
up. Bake until golden brown, about 15 to 20 minutes.

5 Remove the crust from the oven and allow it to cool while you prepare the
pie filling.

6 Increase the oven temperature to 400° F.

7 Melt the butter, while gradually adding the sugar.

8 In a small bowl, beat the eggs lightly, and then add the vinegar, cornmeal, and
vanilla. Gradually add the egg mixture to the butter-and-sugar mixture.

9 Pour into the pie shell and bake for 10 minutes, then lower the temperature to
350° F and continue baking for an additional 35 to 45 minutes, or until the filling is set. Remove the pie from the oven and allow to cool before serving.

Coconut Macaroons
～ *Joyce Goldstein* ～

Joyce Goldstein's granddaughter Elena loves these cookies, and Joyce says they remind her "of a Mounds Bar, only better." She recommends eating them with coconut ice cream and hot fudge sauce and challenges anyone to stop after they've had just one. Among her grandchildren's favorites, these are at the top of the list.

MAKES 4 TO 5 DOZEN COOKIES

5 egg whites

1⅓ cups sugar

5 cups toasted unsweetened coconut

½ tablespoon vanilla

8 ounces bittersweet chocolate, melted

1 Preheat the oven to 275° F. Line two cookie sheets with parchment paper.

2 Beat the egg whites to soft peaks. Gradually beat in the sugar. Fold in the coconut and vanilla.

3 Using a pastry bag, pipe the macaroons out onto the cookie sheets, about 2 inches apart. If you don't have a pastry bag and tip, you can scoop the mixture out using a tablespoon. The cookies should be about 1 inch in diameter. Bake for 20 minutes. The macaroons should still be moist inside and white outside. Allow the cookies to cool.

4 Dip the bottom of each cookie in melted chocolate. The chocolate takes about 3 hours to set. Store in an airtight container.

⊰ KITCHEN MEMORIES ⊱

Family meals and holiday meals are very important to us. Even the night before Thanksgiving, when my former son-in-law and I peel chestnuts together for the stuffing, is a tradition. He and my daughter Rachel have been divorced for ten years, and we still do the chestnuts every Thanksgiving Eve because that's part of our tradition. We even have an annual Oscar party. I use it as a forum to test recipes on my family. I can't imagine our getting together without food and wine. Sitting around a table with your family is very important.

Rhubarb Pie
⪻ Gale Gand ⪼
TRU, CHICAGO

Gale Gand didn't start thinking about having a family until she was thirty-six years old. Not long after she realized that she "forgot to have kids," she and her first husband, Ric Tramonto, conceived their son, Gio, and started a family. Gale has some wonderful memories of making this pie with Gio.

MAKES ONE 9-INCH PIE

1 recipe Plain and Perfect Pie Crust
  (recipe follows)
6 cups rhubarb, leaves and brown edges
  trimmed off, cut into 1-inch slices
  (about 14 stalks)

½ cup plus 1 tablespoon sugar
¼ cup cornstarch
1½ tablespoons cold unsalted butter,
  cut into pieces
1 tablespoon heavy cream

1 Preheat the oven to 425° F.

2 Roll out two crusts; fit one in the bottom of a 10-inch pie pan and place the other on a sheet pan (for the top crust). Refrigerate both crusts.

3 In a large bowl, toss the rhubarb, ½ cup of sugar, and cornstarch together. Transfer to the bottom pie shell. Dot with the cut-up butter. Brush the overhanging edges of the dough with water. Carefully place the rolled-out top crust on top and pinch the edges together; trim the dough so the overhang is 1 inch. Turn the edge under all around to make a thick edge. To decorate the rim, just press it all around with the back of a fork. For a slightly more sophisticated look, press the thumb and forefinger of one hand together. Use them to gently push the thick dough rim outward, while pushing inward with the forefinger of the other hand, so that they intersect in a V with the dough in between. Repeat all around the rim to make a wavy edge.

4 With the tips of a pair of scissors, snip 4 evenly spaced small vent holes in the top crust. Brush the top of the pie with cream, then sprinkle evenly with the remaining tablespoon of sugar.

5 Place the pie on a sheet pan to catch any juices that boil over. Bake in the center of the oven for 10 minutes, then reduce the heat to 375° F and bake until

the crust is golden brown and the juices are bubbling at the vents, 40 to 50 minutes more. Check the pie after 30 minutes; if the crust is browning too quickly, cover it lightly with foil.

6 Let cool for at least 30 minutes before serving. Serve warm or at room temperature.

PLAIN AND PERFECT PIE CRUST

MAKES ENOUGH FOR TWO SINGLE-CRUST PIES OR ONE DOUBLE-CRUST PIE

4½ cups sifted all-purpose flour
2 teaspoons kosher salt
2 teaspoons sugar
12 ounces (3 sticks) unsalted
   butter, cold, cut into pieces

½ cup ice water (strain out the ice
   just before using)
2 teaspoons red wine vinegar

1 In a mixer fitted with a paddle attachment (or using a hand mixer), mix the flour, salt, and sugar for 1 minute. Add the butter and mix just until you have a crumbly, sandy mixture. You should still be able to see pieces of butter.

2 In a small bowl, stir the water and vinegar together. With the mixer running at medium speed, drizzle in the water-vinegar mixture and mix just until a dough forms. You should still see small bits of butter.

3 Turn out onto a work surface, divide the dough in half, and shape into round, flat disks. Wrap each separately in plastic wrap and refrigerate for at least 30 minutes or up to 48 hours. (If you need only 1 crust, freeze the second disk of dough for up to 1 month. Thaw in the refrigerator overnight before rolling out.)

4 When the time comes to roll out the dough, let the dough warm up for a few minutes so it doesn't crack when you start to roll it. Dust a work surface with a few tablespoons of flour, and keep some extra flour at hand. Sprinkle a little flour on top of the dough and start rolling outward from the center with quick, light strokes. Don't worry if the edges split a bit; concentrate on getting a good circle going from the center. Lift up and rotate the dough one-quarter turn every minute or so to help ensure even rolling. The dough should feel smooth and soft; some say it should feel like the inside of your forearm. If it gets sticky, sprinkle on a bit more flour, but don't do this more than two or three times, or the dough will

absorb too much flour and will be tough instead of buttery and flaky. Instead, put it back in the fridge for 15 minutes to firm the butter up. Keep rolling until the circle is at least 2 inches larger than your pan (for example, 11 inches wide for a 9-inch pie pan), or 3 inches larger for deep-dish pies.

5 Set your pie or tart pan nearby. I always use heavy aluminum pans because glass pans seem to bake the crust too fast. To transfer the crust to the pan, I find it easiest to roll a finished crust up onto the rolling pin, and gently unroll it in the pan. Or, you can fold it gently in quarters, lift it up, position the center point on the center of the pan, and unfold it into the pan. Make sure that the dough is allowed to settle completely into the pan. Don't stretch and press the dough into the corners; stretched dough is likely to shrink back when you bake it. Instead, lift the edges of the crust to let it settle down into the corners. If the dough tears a bit, don't be concerned; it can be patched. Using scissors or a sharp knife, trim the dough to within ¾ inch of the rim. Use any extra scraps to patch the crust, pressing with your fingers (wet them if necessary); set aside.

For a double-crust pie: Leave the edges of the bottom crust hanging over the rim. Roll out the second piece of dough into a circle about 11 inches in diameter. Line a sheet pan with parchment or wax paper. Roll the dough up onto the rolling pin, then unroll it onto the sheet pan. Refrigerate the finished crust or crusts for 20 to 30 minutes before filling the pie. When the bottom crust is filled, rest the top crust on top and pinch the edges together, turning them under all the way around. To decorate the rim, just press it all around with the back of a fork. For a slightly more sophisticated look, press the thumb and forefinger of one hand together. Use them to gently push the thick dough rim outward, while pushing inward with the forefinger of the other hand, so that they intersect in a "V" with the dough in between. Repeat all around the rim to make a wavy edge.

For a prebaked pie or tart crust: Preheat the oven to 375° F. Line the inside of the chilled crust with aluminum foil. Don't turn it down over the rim, but leave the extra sticking up so that you have something to hold on to. Fill the foil all the way up to the top of the shell with pie weights or dried beans. Bake for 25 to 30 minutes, until dry and beginning to turn "blond." Lift the foil and weights out of the shell and bake for another 10 to 15 minutes, checking frequently to prevent overbaking, until medium brown.

Amy's Mom's Whole Lemon Pie
Amy Scherber
AMY'S BREAD, NEW YORK

It seems incongruous that Amy Scherber, owner/operator of the New York City's famed Amy's Bread, could have grown up eating Pillsbury convenience products, but she did. Her father worked for the company, and while her mother made canned cinnamon buns often for breakfast, she loved to cook and would experiment with something new every day. The whole family would sit down together every night for dinner, an important part of the daily ritual. As a young girl, Amy often hung out in the kitchen helping her mother and chatting about food. When she was thirteen, her mother began teaching her how to make the things her family liked to eat.

Her mother's early instructions helped prepare her for the job she took as a private cook and housekeeper when she was twenty. She had no idea what she was getting herself into and spent a lot of time studying cookbooks. Always around food in one way or another, she waited tables and worked in the front of the house until 1987, when she enrolled in the New York Restaurant School. There she discovered baking and, preferring savory to sweet, went to France for a few months to learn about bread. She came back home with a head full of ideas and she soon felt confident enough to take a job at Mondrian in New York City, where she created her own formulas and starters and found an inspirational mentor in Tom Colicchio who "had a good sense about bread." After two years at Mondrian she worked up the nerve to open her own bakery. After just four years she needed more space and expanded to a second location. Most recently she added a retail shop with a café and now oversees 110 employees. Amy is newly married and recently became a mom. She hopes that little Harry will grow up with an admiration for food and a love of flavors and ingredients just as she did.

Mom's Secret Be sure the lemon is very finely ground. A blender works much better than a food processor. If the lemon rind is still in small bits, the pie will be overwhelmed with the flavor of lemon zest. Since the entire lemon, including the rind, is being used you might consider buying organic lemons.

This pie is quick, easy, and a real crowd-pleaser. Amy recommends using a Meyer lemon, a variety often preferred by chefs and passionate home cooks because it is slightly sweeter than the more common Lisbon and Eureka varieties. When fully ripe, a Meyer lemon will have a slightly orange hue and a hint of tangerine flavor.

1 large or 2 small Meyer lemons
4 eggs
1½ cups sugar

1 stick (4 ounces) unsalted butter, softened
1 teaspoon vanilla extract
1 (9-inch) unbaked pie crust (see page 172)

1 Preheat the oven to 350°F.

2 Wash the lemon, trim off the ends, and cut into eighths lengthwise. Remove the seeds and trim off any thick pith.

3 Place the lemon in the blender. Puree on high until very finely pulverized.

4 Add the eggs and sugar and blend again.

5 Add the soft butter and vanilla and blend again until fully combined and smooth.

6 Pour the filling into the prepared pie crust.

7 Bake for 40 minutes, or until the center is set but still slightly soft.

8 Cool completely before serving.

⊰ KITCHEN MEMORIES ⊱

I remember that around the age of thirteen, a friend of mine and I decided we were going to make an elaborate African dinner for all of our friends. We got cookbooks at the library and made all this food like cold buttermilk soup that had strange ingredients. We made elaborate bread and some lamb, and my mother sort of coached us along. Everyone thought our food was so good that I wanted to keep cooking, so Mom taught me how to make all the different recipes that our family liked. I remember her teaching me how to make spaghetti sauce, which I really liked because you could do a little improvisation—you could add a little more onion or a little more tomato paste and chunks of tomato. You don't use a recipe, you taste it to see if it's right, so it was the first time I figured out what would taste good and how to smell good flavor. Mom made baked goods and always had recipes for that, but the rest, she would just cook from the top of her head. She had something for dessert every night—cookies, bars, or pie, or I'd make ice cream sundaes for everyone with all their special requests. We had lots of different nuts and canned whipped cream. We did that for many years. It's surprising that none of us is very fat, but we were very active and Mom made healthy food.

Pecan Sticky Buns
Amy Scherber
AMY'S BREAD, NEW YORK

MAKES 16 BUNS

1 envelope active dry yeast

¼ cup very warm water (105° to 115°F)

5⅓ cups unbleached all-purpose flour

2 cups warm water (90°F)

2¼ teaspoons kosher salt

Flavorless vegetable oil as needed
  for oiling bowl

1⅛ cups (2¼ sticks) unsalted butter,
  plus an additional 4 to 6 tablespoons
  unsalted butter, softened

1 cup plus 2 tablespoons firmly packed
  dark brown sugar

1 cup pecan pieces, toasted

⅓ cup plus 1 tablespoon granulated sugar

1 teaspoon ground cinnamon

1 Combine the yeast and warm water in bowl and stir to dissolve the yeast. Let stand for 3 minutes. Add the flour, second amount of warm water, and salt to the yeast and warm water mixture and mix until it gathers into a shaggy mass.

2 Move the dough to a lightly floured surface and knead for 5 minutes. This is a soft, moist dough. If it seems too stiff and is hard to knead, add extra warm water 1 tablespoon at a time until the dough gets softer. Gently shape the dough into a loose ball, cover it with oiled plastic wrap, and let it rest on the table for 20 minutes.

3 Gently knead the dough for 1 to 2 more minutes until it becomes smooth, supple, and elastic, but not too firm. Shape the dough into a loose ball, place it in a lightly oiled bowl, and turn to coat with oil. Cover and let it rise at room temperature (75° to 77° F) until it has doubled in volume, 1½ to 2 hours.

4 While the dough is rising, combine the 2¼ sticks of butter and the dark brown sugar in a small saucepan over low heat, stirring occasionally, until the butter has melted and the sugar is completely moistened (it won't be dissolved). Whisk until the mixture looks silky and a little lighter in color. Remove from the heat. Use 1 tablespoon of the softened butter to grease the sides of two baking pans (one 9 x 13-inch and one 8 x 5-inch loaf pan), then pour in the caramel, tilting the pan slightly so the mixture spreads evenly over the bottom of each pan. Sprinkle the toasted pecans over the warm caramel and press them down slightly. Put the pans in the refrigerator to cool the caramel; be sure the pans are on a level surface.

5 Put the granulated sugar and cinnamon in a small bowl and stir until evenly mixed. Set aside. When the dough has doubled, gently pour it out of the bowl onto a floured work surface. Flatten the dough and stretch it with your fingers to form a 13 x 10-inch rectangle, with a long side facing you. Work gently so you don't tear the dough. The dough should stretch easily at this point, but if it resists, let it rest for 5 minutes and resume stretching. Check to be sure the dough isn't sticking to the work surface, and flour the table again if necessary.

6 Spread the remaining softened butter evenly over the dough, leaving a ½-inch strip unbuttered along the top edge. Sprinkle the cinnamon-sugar mixture generously and evenly over the butter, again leaving the top ½ inch of the rectangle bare. Starting with the bottom edge, roll up the dough jelly-roll fashion into a long log; if the dough sticks to the table as you're rolling, use a dough scraper to loosen it gently. Pinch gently but firmly along the seam to seal it. If necessary, gently shape the roll so it is a nice uniform log.

7 Cut the log of dough into sixteen equal pieces. (It's easiest to mark the roll first to show where you're going to make the cuts—a slight indentation with the knife edge will do—then use a sharp serrated knife to cut completely through the dough.) Lay the pieces cut-sides down on the top of the cooled caramel in the baking pan, twelve rolls in the large pan and four in the loaf pan. Don't worry if it's a tight fit. Let rise, uncovered, at room temperature until the dough has almost doubled, 1 to 1¼ hours. The rolls should fill the pan and rise almost to the top of the 9x13 pan, and slightly below the top of the loaf pan.

8 As the rolls rise, position a rack in the center of the oven and preheat the oven to 375° F. Put the pans of sticky buns on a baking sheet and place it in the oven. Bake for 10 minutes, then reduce the oven temperature to 350° F and bake for 30 to 40 minutes longer, until the tops of the buns are golden brown and crusty. It's important to bake the buns long enough so the dough is cooked all the way through and the caramel topping develops properly.

9 Set the pans of buns on a rack to cool for 5 minutes. Then quickly but carefully turn each pan upside down and release the sticky buns onto a large, flat, heatproof plate. Immediately scrape out any hot caramel remaining in the bottom of the pans and spread it on the tops of the buns, filling in any bare spots. Let them cool until just warm before serving. (Clean the pans by soaking them in very hot water to dissolve the caramel.) Store any leftovers covered with plastic wrap at room temperature.

Chocolate Chip Cookies
❧ Emily Luchetti ❧
FARALLON, SAN FRANCISCO

Just about every mom has a recipe for chocolate chip cookies—even in today's world of packaged foods. Emily Luchetti's mother timed her baking so that there were warm cookies just out of the oven when Emily came home from school. "If I had to give up all the desserts and could keep only one, I'd keep the chocolate chip cookie," Emily claims. This recipe is guaranteed to transport you back to the warmest moments of your childhood, and it might even replace your current chocolate chip recipe! (The copious amount of vanilla might be the secret.)

MAKES 30 COOKIES

8 ounces (16 tablespoons or 2 sticks) unsalted butter, softened

1 cup firmly packed brown sugar

1 cup granulated sugar

2 large eggs

1 tablespoon vanilla extract

2½ cups all-purpose flour

1 teaspoon baking soda

½ teaspoon salt

2½ cups semisweet chocolate chips

1 Preheat the oven to 350° F.

2 In a mixing bowl, cream the butter and the sugars together until light and creamy.

3 Add the eggs one at a time, beating well after each addition. Add vanilla and mix well.

4 Mix in the dry ingredients and the chocolate chips.

5 Scoop the cookie dough into 1½-inch balls and chill for 30 minutes.

6 Place the balls on parchment-lined baking sheets several inches apart.

7 Bake for about 15 minutes, until golden brown. Cool slightly before removing them from the baking sheet.

Coffee Icebox Cake
❧ *Susan Feniger* ❧
BORDER GRILL, SANTA MONICA AND LAS VEGAS
CIUDAD, LOS ANGELES

Susan Feniger grew up in Toledo, Ohio, which she describes as "not the culinary capital of the world," but she had a mother who had confidence in the kitchen and loved to use strong flavors in her cooking, setting the stage for Susan's fiery and flavorful culinary career. Today she operates the famous Border Grill and Ciudad with her partner Mary Sue Milliken. This icebox cake recipe comes right out of Susan's childhood. Her mother always had something on hand in the freezer for drop-in guests, and this cake was part of her repertoire.

SERVES 8 TO 12

1½ dozen lady fingers	1 pint heavy cream
40 marshmallows	¼ pound toasted almonds
1 cup strong coffee	

1 Lightly butter an 8-inch springform pan and line with ladyfingers.

2 In a double boiler, melt the marshmallows in the hot coffee, then cool.

3 Whip the cream into soft peaks and fold into the cooled coffee-and-marshmallow mixture.

4 Fill the mold with the mixture and top with the toasted almonds. Freeze until semifrozen. To serve, unmold onto a platter and slice.

⊰ KITCHEN MEMORIES ⊱

My mother did these frozen icebox cakes and cheesecakes for dessert all the time, with ladyfingers and coffee mousse or chocolate mousse. One time, when Mary Sue and I had City Café, she made eight icebox cakes, froze them, had my father pack them in dry ice, and shipped them out for us to sell at the café. It was too funny that she'd go to the extreme of shipping these delicate, frozen cakes from Chicago to California. They were delicious. They're not something you think about doing in a restaurant, but we sold all eight of them!

Ginger Cake with Honey-Glazed Peaches
❧ *Jody Adams* ❧
RIALTO, CAMBRIDGE, MASSACHUSETTS ❖ BLU, BOSTON

Jody Adams (pictured with her daughter, opposite) told us that this cake was "born out of necessity" when late one summer evening she and her family found themselves with most of the fixings for a cake, including lots of peaches and some candied ginger, but no baking powder. She said, "We did have yeast. My sister and I knew what to do, just as we had in our childhood—we improvised. Our family has a basic butter cake recipe that we use all year round—changing the fruit, adding nuts, and adjusting the spices according to the season. We took that recipe, consulted the *Joy of Cooking*, and put together the first draft of this cake. It wasn't perfect, but everyone said it was delicious and ate it up. Later I poked and prodded to get it right."

SERVES 8

1 envelope active dry yeast	½ cup plus 1 tablespoon unsalted
6 tablespoons milk	butter, at room temperature
2 cups plus 1 tablespoon unbleached	2 large eggs
all-purpose flour	1 teaspoon grated lemon zest
3 firm ripe peaches, cut in half, pits	½ cup honey
removed	¼ cup minced crystallized ginger
1 cup sugar	1 tablespoon ground ginger
1 tablespoon freshly squeezed lemon juice	1 teaspoon kosher salt

1 Preheat the oven to 350°.

2 Whisk the yeast in the milk. Stir in ½ cup of flour. Allow to sit for 30 minutes in a warm place.

3 Cut the peaches into quarters and toss with ¼ cup of sugar and the lemon juice.

4 Grease a 9-inch springform pan with 1 tablespoon of butter, then dust it with tablespoon of flour.

5 Cream the remaining ½ cup of butter in a large bowl with the remaining ¾ cup of sugar until light and fluffy. Add the eggs, one at a time, until well com-

bined. Add the yeast mixture to the butter mixture. Beat in the lemon zest, 6 tablespoons of the honey, and 2 tablespoons of crystallized ginger.

6 Mix in the remaining 1½ cups of flour with the ground ginger and salt. Stir into the butter mixture.

7 Scrape the batter into the prepared pan. Put two peach quarters in the center, then arrange the remaining peaches in circles around the edge. Allow to rise for 30 minutes. Bake for 45 minutes or until done. (The cake should be golden brown on top, and a toothpick inserted into the cake—not the peaches—should come out clean.) Sprinkle with the remaining crystallized ginger and drizzle with the remaining honey. Let cool for 10 minutes before removing the sides of the springform pan and serving.

Swedish Apple Pie
≈ Debra Ponzek ≈
AUX DELICES FOODS, RIVERSIDE, CONNECTICUT

Debra Ponzek's mother took French cooking classes shortly after she married, so although Debra was growing up in a typical middle-class convenience-food-loving American home, her mother mixed it up a little with some finer and more interesting dishes from time to time. Debra credits her mother with her own love of French cooking, which is evident in her menus today. She was also influenced by her grandmother, with whom she started cooking when she was about nine years old. With her she learned how to make bread and a variety of baked goods from her Polish heritage. As a young adult she entered engineering school, but a couple of years into the program at Boston University, she realized she just wasn't cut out for it and decided to try her luck at the Culinary Institute of America. She "loved every minute of it, from the first day to the last." After culinary school while working in New Jersey, Debra heard that there was a job opening at Montrachet. She applied, was hired, and ten months later, when the chef quit, she was promoted to take his position and catapulted to stardom. In fact, Debra was the first woman chef in New York to earn three stars from the *New York Times*. She remained there for eight years and left to write a book, get married, and start a family. She and her new husband moved to Connecticut and bought their first home. In the first nine years after she left Montrachet, Debra and her husband started three businesses and had three children. The children, now eight, seven, and four, are growing up with a real connection to food and the restaurant business, as they spend more and more time in the recently expanded kitchens of Aux Delices Foods near their Greenwich, Connecticut, home.

At home they like to help make eggs and pancakes, pizzas and pasta, and, of course, cookies—the kinds of foods all kids like—but Debra is determined to give them as much culinary exposure as possible. Even if they don't actually taste a food or an herb, she asks them to at least smell it, hoping that the information thus imparted will stick with them as their palates grow and change.

This Swedish Apple Pie is something Debra's mother used to make for her when she was a young girl. Debra (pictured here with her children) uses the same recipe today.

SERVES 8 TO 12

7 **Golden Delicious apples**
½ **cup raisins**
1 **stick (4 ounces) unsalted butter**
¾ **cup sugar**
1 **egg**
1 **cup plus** ¼ **cup all-purpose flour**

TOPPING
3 **teaspoons sugar**
1 **teaspoon cinnamon**
¼ **cup chopped walnuts (optional)**

1 Preheat the oven to 350° F.

2 Peel and slice the apples into ¼-inch slices. Cover the bottom of a deep 9-inch pie plate with the apple slices. Sprinkle with the raisins.

3 In a mixing bowl on medium speed, cream together the butter and sugar until light and fluffy. Add the egg and then the cup of flour and mix well. Remove from the bowl onto a surface that is sprinkled with ¼ cup of flour. Work the flour into the dough as you flatten the crust. Lightly pat the crust into a flat piece that is about ¼ to ½ inch thick. Cut the crust into 2 x 2-inch pieces. Lay them over the apples to create a "patchwork" effect.

4 Combine the topping ingredients and mix well. Sprinkle the topping over the crust and bake for 45 to 50 minutes, until the crust is golden brown and the apples are bubbly.

Grandma's Orange Slice Cookies
❧ *Coleen Donnelly* ❧

Not only do the ingredients in this recipe combine to create wonderful flavor, but they're also a lot of fun to make. Since the orange slice candies have to be cut into tiny pieces before mixing them in with the cookie dough, this is a great recipe to do with children who are able to handle a pair of scissors. Coleen's grandmother (pictured below) used to make these, and Coleen says she's never seen a recipe like this one anywhere since. She used to serve them at her former restaurant, Magnolia, and intends to put them on a cookie plate as a tribute to her grandmother in the future.

MAKES 2 TO 3 DOZEN COOKIES, DEPENDING ON SIZE

1 cup granulated sugar
1 cup brown sugar
½ cup vegetable shortening
¼ pound (1 stick) unsalted butter
2 eggs
1 teaspoon vanilla extract
1 teaspoon milk
2 cups all-purpose flour

1 teaspoon baking soda
1 teaspoon baking powder
¼ teaspoon salt
1 cup chopped walnuts
1 pound orange slice candy, snipped
    into ¼-inch pieces (sharp scissors
    work well)
2 cups rolled oats

1 Preheat the oven to 350° F.

2 In the bowl of an electric mixer, cream the sugars, shortening, and butter.

3 Add the eggs, one at a time, mixing well to incorporate between additions. Add vanilla and milk and stir to combine.

4 In a small bowl combine the flour, baking soda, baking powder, and salt and add to the butter-sugar-egg mixture. Mix to blend.

5 When just blended, add the walnuts, candy slices, and oats.

6 Drop by rounded teaspoons onto an ungreased cookie sheet and bake until the cookie edges brown. Take care not to overcook; the cookies should be slightly chewy.

⊰ KITCHEN MEMORIES ⊱

People say that I have an excellent palate, which is a compliment I appreciate. But I've always thought a good palate must be like the ability to play the piano or the violin. I don't think it's something you're born with, but something you learn because my mother, my sister, and my grandmother, all have excellent palates and it's because my grandmother taught us all what good food should taste like. When she put food in front of us, it was the way it's supposed to taste. She made her own pasta for chicken and dumplings and her own bread, as did her mother. If I smell meat that has been properly seasoned, seared, and roasted, I am instantly transported to my grandmother's house and to her kitchen, and the memory is huge. When I think about the scrambled eggs she used to make that were so perfect, I don't know what she did, but it was heaven, they were magic. And I remember just wanting more and more and more of them. She made this apple cake so crispy on the outside and perfectly tender and appley on the inside.

There are a lot of ways that different foods taste, but proper technique is proper technique and that only tastes one way. I understand that my palate was created by the people who fed me every day. I'm lucky to have those food memories.

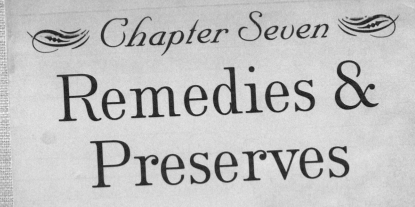

Chapter Seven
Remedies & Preserves

HOME REMEDIES AND PRESERVES both seem to have some mystical power. Chicken soup, like Lisa Schroeder's Belle's Chicken Noodle Soup, is made up of just a few ingredients, yet, it can cure just about anything that ails. Gale Gand's Mom's Sore Throat Remedy has only two ingredients—butter and honey—yet it works like magic. Preserving and canning seem sort of magical to most of us in today's world. Fresh fruit can be turned into jam—like Bonnie Moore's unbelievably smooth Red Raspberry–Vanilla Jam or Stephanie Kimmel's delectable Aunt Sis's Tomato Preserves—that lasts a year in a jar in the pantry. Everyone has their own quirky method and approach to the process, and the tools may vary as much as cooking times. Hilary Demane makes Grape Conserve using a special grape-gathering bag that's been passed down for generations, almost as though there's something about the bag itself that contributes to the process. Who knows? Maybe there is something mystical about chasing away an illness with food or capturing the essence of summer in a jar, but if you follow the recipes in this chapter, you're sure to have great success in the kitchen. All of these recipes will be a big hit with your family, whether they're sick or just plain hungry for something deliciously homemade.

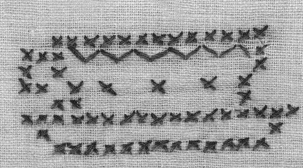

Belle's Chicken Noodle Soup
Lisa Schroeder

MOTHER'S BISTRO & BAR, PORTLAND, OREGON

Lisa Schroeder (pictured with her daughter, page 190) has special memories of her mother's chicken soup. She always made it for the Jewish holidays, so there was never a question as to what the signature soup would be at Lisa's restaurant, Mother's Bistro. It's offered there with a choice of egg noodles or matzo balls, and devotees know when it's time for their fix—a sniffly nose, a slight cough, or just a need for comfort. Sometimes called Jewish penicillin, this soup is simple to make and easily can become Chicken and Dumplings with a few more steps.

SERVES 10

BROTH

2 whole chickens
2 whole onions, peeled
4 stalks celery, rinsed
4 carrots, peeled
4 parsnips, peeled
1 bunch flat-leaf (Italian) parsley,
   stems and all
Salt and freshly ground pepper to taste

SOUP

2 cups finely diced carrots
2 cups finely diced celery
1 recipe Matzo Balls (see below) or
   1 pound of egg noodles
1 bunch fresh dill, chopped, for garnish

1 In a large pot just big enough to hold the chickens (about 10- to 12-quart capacity), put in the chicken, onions, celery, carrots, parsnips, and parsley. Use a tall, narrow pot, rather than a wide one, and fill with just enough water to barely cover the chickens. Bring to a boil and skim any scum that rises to the surface. Turn down the heat so the broth simmers. Rapid boiling of any soup or stock will usually lead to a cloudy, not clear, soup.

2 Season lightly with salt and pepper (You'll season again later. You're seasoning here because you want the chicken meat to have some flavor.)

3 Simmer the broth, uncovered, for at least 2 to 3 hours. Taste it and you'll know if it's ready. Does it taste like chicken? If not, let it go a bit longer and taste again. If you forget about it for another hour or two, it shouldn't be a problem, as long

as it is barely simmering. Once the soup is done, turn off the heat, lift the chicken from the pot, and set it aside until cool enough to handle.

4 Strain the broth into a clean 6- to 8-quart pot. You can discard (or nibble on) the strained-out parsnip, carrots, celery, and onion, because they have done their job and are not included in the final plated dish.

5 Add the finely diced carrots and celery to the pot with the strained broth, which will add color, flavor, and texture to the final plated soup.

6 Cook the vegetables in the uncovered simmering broth until just tender.

7 Taste the soup and adjust the seasoning with salt and freshly ground pepper, if necessary.

8 While the vegetables are cooking, pick the meat off the chicken, trying to leave the pieces as large as possible. Discard the bones. Set aside.

9 Make Matzo Balls (recipe follows), or cook the egg noodles according to the package directions. When the the noodles are cooked through, strain them through a colander, shock them (stop the cooking with cold water), drain, and set aside.

10 Add 2 cups cooked noodles or matzo balls to serving bowls. Ladle broth, chicken, and vegetables into the bowls, sprinkle with fresh chopped dill, and serve.

KITCHEN MEMORIES

When my daughter, Stephanie, was sick, we'd have our routine—first stop was the doctor, then to the pharmacy to get the prescribed medicine, and finally to the supermarket, where we'd pick up the ingredients for the chicken soup. Once home, the simmering soup was on the stove within fifteen minutes. Sure, it wasn't ready for a few more hours after that, but we ate it for days and loved every meal made with it.

MATZO BALLS

Makes 1 dozen

¼ cup chicken fat, melted but not hot (you can use the chicken fat that rises to the top of the chicken soup as it cools)

7 eggs, beaten

7 tablespoons broth from Belle's Chicken Noodle Soup *(above)*

7 tablespoons soda water

½ pound matzo meal (found in the kosher section of the supermarket)

½ tablespoon salt

1 In a large mixing bowl, whisk together the chicken fat and eggs. Add the chicken soup, soda water, matzo meal, and salt and mix just enough to combine. Cover the bowl and place in the refrigerator for 30 minutes.

2 Bring a large (8- to 10-quart) pot of salted water to a boil. Remove the matzo ball mixture from the refrigerator. Using a small ice cream scoop, take a scoop of the mixture. With wet hands, shape each scoop into a ball, then drop the balls in the boiling water. Once all the balls have been shaped and dropped into the water, make sure it comes back to a boil. Lower the heat to a simmer, cover, and cook for 30 minutes.

3 If serving the matzo balls immediately, place one or two in each soup bowl, then ladle hot soup over them and serve garnished with fresh chopped dill. If making ahead, remove the pot from the heat, and set aside to cool a bit. Lift the balls out of the water with a slotted spoon, place in a storage container, and add just enough cooking liquid to cover the matzo balls. Refrigerate. To serve, lift the matzo balls out of their cooking liquid and place them in a pot with the chicken soup. Bring to a boil over medium-high heat; lower the heat and simmer for 8 minutes, or until the matzo balls are heated through. Serve as suggested above.

Mom's Sore Throat Remedy
⇒ *Gale Gand* ⇒
TRU, CHICAGO

Gale's mom (pictured with Gale, above) used to mix honey and butter together as a sore throat remedy. You may be more familiar with the traditional honey-and-lemon remedy, but Gale swears by this instead. Gale's mother also made a matzo ball soup that could cure anything, and she's a big fan of root-beer floats as an all-purpose remedy. Gale even makes and sells her own line of root beers. Kids seem to like this recipe better than honey and lemon, so next time one of yours gets a sore throat, give it a try!

4 tablespoons (½ stick) unsalted butter, at room temperature   **2 tablespoons honey**

Combine the two ingredients into a smooth paste and eat by the spoonful to soothe a sore throat. Keep in a jar, refrigerated, for future use.

Grandmother Keck's Floating Island
❧ Katy Keck ❧
THE NEW WORLD GRILL, NEW YORK

This is the delectable treat that was bestowed upon sick children in Katy Keck's (pictured with her grandmother, opposite) family when they were sick—with the exception of at least one case that Katy can remember (see opposite)! We're not sure how it works as a cure-all, but it's a great, and classic, dessert—rich, simple, and delicious! Katy says, "If this dessert doesn't cheer you up, nothing will!"

SERVES 4, UNLESS THE PEOPLE YOU'RE SERVING ARE SICK

2 cups milk
3 eggs, separated
½ cup sugar

⅛ teaspoon salt
⅛ teaspoon vanilla extract
Colored sprinkles for garnish

1 In a large saucepan, scald the milk.

2 Using a wire whisk, or in the bowl of an electric mixer, beat the egg whites until stiff. Slowly beat in half of the granulated sugar to create a meringue.

3 Drop the meringue by large spoonfuls into the milk. Poach gently—do not boil—for 2 minutes. Turn each meringue once and poach for an additional 2 minutes.

4 Remove the meringues from the milk using a slotted spoon or spatula, and drain on a towel. Refrigerate meringues on a plate. Transfer the poaching milk to the top of a double boiler, but do not put it over the heat.

5 Beat the egg yolks and slowly, in a thin stream, stir them into the milk along with the remaining ¼ cup of sugar and salt to make a custard. It is very important not to add the eggs too quickly, or you will end up with lumpy custard.

6 Place the custard over boiling water and stir constantly until the mixture begins to thicken. Once thickened, remove it from the heat and continue beating until it stops steaming. Stir in the vanilla extract.

7 Divide the custard into four custard cups and chill. When the custards are cool, place a meringue on top of each one and refrigerate.

8 Before serving, sprinkle each floating island with colored sprinkles, which will run on the meringue, giving it a confetti look.

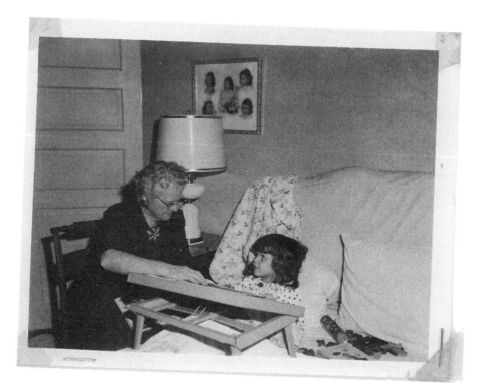

Blackberry–Grand Marnier Sauce
Bonnie Moore

THE FOODFIT COMPANY (FOODFIT.COM), WASHINGTON, D.C.

Bonnie Moore credits her mother and father equally with her interest in food. Her mother grew up on a farm in Nova Scotia, so she was able to teach Bonnie what it meant to have high-quality produce, and she knew how to make things last. She also knew a lot about fish, having lived so near to the ocean. Her father, on the other hand, was a true gourmand. He loved to eat, traveled a great deal, and enjoyed getting to know a place through its food. At home, Bonnie and her parents cooked and cooked and cooked, often attempting to replicate dishes that they'd eaten at restaurants. When Bonnie announced her decision to be a chef, both of her parents were "aghast." She, on the other hand, thought it was a perfectly natural choice and was equally aghast at their reaction.

After completing cooking school, Bonnie got a job at The Inn at Little Washington making, to her father's horror, seven dollars an hour. When Bonnie was promoted to sous-chef at The Inn, her father finally came around. After three years there, she and her husband moved to Washington D.C., where she took a teaching job at L'Academie Culinaire. Not accustomed to a "short" (thirty-five- to forty-hour) work week, she got antsy and started looking around for supplemental employment. She began working with Ellen Haas on a book and then later took a position at Haas's FoodFit Company, which promotes and supports a healthy lifestyle through fitness and nutrition. Bonnie still works for FoodFit part time, does special events for The Inn at Little Washington, and is the chef of a company called Global Food and Nutrition, which focuses on helping people in Third World countries understand how to get better nutrition. On top of all of that, Bonnie is a new mother, and she can't wait for her son to get his first taste of ice cream!

It will be a while, of course, before he uses this sauce, which Bonnie loves to eat with rich chocolate ice cream. It's also delicious over fresh fruit, alongside panna cotta, or swirled into yogurt.

A NOTE ON CANNING

Home canning/preserving is a very simple and healthful process, providing you follow some basic canning guidelines: We strongly recommend the use of a canning kettle—basically a big pot that comes with a rack to keep the jars off the bottom of the pot and a handle to make removal of the jars from boiling water easy and safe. The jars should never be tipped or tilted as you remove them from the water. They should always be kept upright until the jars are completely sealed and cooled to avoid breaking the seal (which would allow bacteria to get in the jar and contaminate the food). Jars and lids must be sterilized according to the manufacturer's instructions. Always process the jars as long as indicated in the recipe. All the recipes in this book are for altitudes up to 1,000 feet. If you're at a higher altitude consult the USDA for processing times. Always check to make sure your lids have sealed properly. If some have failed to seal, check manufacturer's directions to see if it is possible to reprocess jars that haven't sealed. If not, store those jars in the refrigerator and consume them within a week. Do not make any ingredient substitutions with these recipes. For more information (especially with regard to low acid foods, which require additional acid), consult the USDA (www.usda.gov) and its recommended websites.

MAKES 2 HALF-PINTS

3 cups fresh blackberries
½ cup sugar

1 tablespoon fresh lemon juice
1 tablespoon Grand Marnier

1 In a small heavy-bottomed stainless steel pot, combine the blackberries and sugar. Cook over medium-high heat, stirring occasionally, and boil until the mixture thickens slightly, about 10 to 12 minutes.

2 Remove from the heat and strain through a fine sieve to remove the berry seeds. Add the lemon juice and Grand Marnier.

3 To can (see note above): Pour the sauce into hot, sterilized half-pint jars, leaving ½ inch of headspace. Seal with lids and process in a boiling water bath for 15 minutes. Alternatively, you can freeze the jam instead of canning: Cool the mixture overnight in the refrigerator. Pour into smaller containers, leaving ½ inch of headspace; cover and freeze.

Red Raspberry–Vanilla Jam
❧ *Bonnie Moore* ❧

THE FOOD FIT COMPANY (FOODFIT.COM), WASHINGTON, D.C.

This jam is absolutely divine! Using apple instead of commercial pectin produces a jam with a softer consistency and a beautifully clean, delicious fruit flavor. The vanilla adds a warm toasty flavor and mellows the tartness of the raspberries just perfectly.

MAKES 4 HALF-PINTS

1 Granny Smith apple
5 cups red raspberries
1 tablespoon fresh lemon juice

2 cups sugar
1 vanilla bean, split lengthwise and halved

1 Using a grater, grate the entire apple, including the skin and core but not the seeds.

2 In a large heavy-bottomed stainless steel pot, combine the grated apple, raspberries, and lemon juice. Cook over low heat until the fruit begins to soften. Stir in the sugar and vanilla-bean quarters.

3 Simmer the jam, stirring frequently and skimming any foam that rises to the surface. Cook until the mixture registers 220° F on a candy thermometer, about 10 to 12 minutes. Remove from the heat.

4 To can (see note on page 195): Pour into hot, sterilized half-pint jars (include a piece of vanilla bean in each jar and the vanilla flavor will become stronger), leaving ½ inch of headspace. Seal with lids and process in a boiling water bath for 15 minutes. Alternatively, you can freeze the jam: Cool the mixture overnight in the refrigerator. Pour into smaller containers, leaving ½ inch of headspace; cover and freeze.

Nectarine–Blueberry Jam
✺ *Bonnie Moore* ✺
THE FOOD FIT COMPANY (FOODFIT.COM), WASHINGTON, D.C.

This is another perfectly balanced jam from Bonnie Moore. The combination of nectarines and blueberries is as delicious as it is beautiful.

MAKES 4 HALF-PINTS

1 Granny Smith apple
4 cups peeled, pitted, and sliced
   nectarines

1 cup blueberries
2 tablespoons fresh lemon juice
1¾ cups sugar

1 Using a grater, grate the entire apple, including the skin and core but not the seeds.

2 In a heavy-bottomed stainless steel saucepan, combine the grated apple, nectarines, blueberries, and lemon juice. Cook over low heat until the fruit begins to soften. Stir in the sugar.

3 Simmer the jam, stirring frequently and skimming any foam that rises to the surface. Cook until the mixture registers 220° F on a candy thermometer. Remove from the heat.

4 To can (see note on page 195): Pour into hot, sterilized half-pint jars, leaving ½ inch of headspace. Seal with lids and process in a boiling water bath for 15 minutes. Alternatively, you can freeze the jam: Cool the mixture overnight in the refrigerator. Pour into smaller containers, leaving ½ inch of headspace; cover and freeze.

Pickled Dilled Asparagus
⇜ *Bonnie Moore* ⇝
THE FOOD FIT COMPANY (FOODFIT.COM), WASHINGTON, D.C.

This is great served on a relish tray with cocktails or even in Bloody Marys as an alternative to celery.

MAKES 6 PINTS

4 pounds asparagus

1 teaspoon red pepper flakes

4 teaspoons mustard seeds

4 teaspoons dill seeds

8 cloves garlic

5 cups white wine vinegar

1 Cut the asparagus into lengths that will fit into pint jars. Pack the asparagus into the hot, sterilized jars (tips pointing down) and divide the red pepper flakes, mustard seeds, dill seeds, and garlic among the jars.

2 Combine the vinegar and 5 cups of water in a stainless steel pot and bring to a boil over high heat. Pour the boiling liquid over the asparagus in each jar, filling the jars to within ½ inch of the top.

3 Seal the jars with lids and let process for 15 minutes in a boiling water bath (see note on page 195 about canning).

⇜ KITCHEN MEMORIES ⇝

I have these memories of my mom and my grandmother, both in Nova Scotia and the United States, in the height of the growing season, picking things and putting them up for the winter in various ways. They both had a sense of what the very best of anything was. They knew what should be eaten that night for dinner, what things were overripe or bruised and could be made into the best preserves, and what other things could be frozen so we could, for example, have berry shortcake after the berry season was ended. In the growing season, there were always preserving pots bubbling away and jelly bags dripping in the kitchen. That was what we always did, even though at that point neither my mother nor my grandmother had to do it. It fascinated me how they just knew what to do. They didn't follow a book; they just went about doing it.

Grape Conserve
❧ Hilary Demane ❧

INDIANA UNIVERSITY OF PENNSYLVANIA (IUP), INDIANA, PENNSYLVANIA

When Hilary Demane was growing up, her family always sat down to dinner together, and that couldn't have been easy for Hilary's mom to accomplish, considering the fact that they were a family of seven. To complicate matters the kids always had friends over, and mealtimes were more like one huge adopted family than a small family unit. With a mother of English descent and a father of Italian heritage, their family staple foods were quite varied, but Hilary's mom was also very creative and loved trying new things from the Time/Life series. She did everything from meatloaf and mashed potatoes to beef stroganoff and chocolate mousse. Hilary remembers cooking with her mom as a little girl—especially at breakfast time on Sunday after church, when they frequently made waffles and French toast together. She said, "I can remember helping in the kitchen after school and on the weekends, and then always for holidays, always for holidays, we were always in there. I'll never forget the first time I saw my mother clean a turkey, she reached inside and pulled the innards out. And I said, 'Oh my God, I'm never doing that, Mom, I'll never do that!' She said, 'Oh, honey, I saw my mom do it, and we had to pluck the turkey in those days. You'll do it some day,' and of course, have I stuck my hand inside a turkey since?! How many thousands of turkeys?!" To this day Hilary has no idea how her mother found the time to cook as much as she did.

Hilary currently teaches at the Indiana University of Pennsylvania (IUP), where she has been shaping young culinary minds and palates for more than fifteen years. Prior to that, she taught at a culinary school in Florida and estimates that she has had the good fortune throughout her career to influence literally thousands of students, who she says, have all come to feel like her own children.

This conserve recipe has a long family history. Today Hilary has a Concord grapevine in her garden and this past year had the wonderful experience of picking and cleaning grapes with some of her students as they sat out on the deck in the sunshine of early fall, sharing stories of cooking with their families.

This conserve is more work than plain jelly, but the end result is worth it, and it keeps well, even over longer periods of time. Hilary's family anxiously awaits the grape harvest every year to see if she will be sending jars back home.

8 pounds Concord grapes

8 pounds sugar (Do not decrease this
amount or your conserve will not jell
properly)

1½ pounds raisins

4 oranges, sliced as thinly as possible

2 lemons, sliced as thinly as possible

3 cups pecans, coarsely chopped
(walnuts, black walnuts, or hickory
nuts may also be used)

Mom's Secret Concord grapes are sometimes available in the market in late summer or early fall. If you can pick your own grapes, it is always best to include some that are underripe or pale green because they have more pectin than fully ripe or overripe grapes, which may not jell as well.

⊱ KITCHEN MEMORIES ⊰

I feel like I have a total connection with food from the ground up, because not only did my mother have a garden, but she had a grapevine that my grandmother planted when she came over from England. Every year we would go out and pick the grapes, and we would make grape juice and then make grape jelly, and my mom had this ancient grape bag, which I have now. It's so wonderful that I still have this! We'd make the jelly, put it in the jars, and put it on the windowsill and watch the sun come through, and it was like stained glass—just so exciting. It was nice standing back to look at what we'd made because it was so perfect. To me, that connection, from the ground up, is what I still feel about food. One of the neatest things about my house here in Pennsylvania is that we have a Concord grapevine that someone planted fifty years ago and I still make grape jelly. It's wonderful that I got that from my mom, and it was something special enough to keep alive today. I can pass it on to my students and they can get excited about it.

Every fall to this day my mother asks, "How are the grapes? Have you got a good grape crop? Are you going to have time to do something this year?" I always say that I don't have time, and then I look out there at the grapes and I just can't leave them there. So I always end up, at midnight, saying, "Geez, these damned grapes!" But I love it!

1 Wash the grapes. Remove the skins by gently popping them off in between your thumb and forefinger. Reserve the skins.

2 Cook the grapes in a heavy pot on medium heat until they are soft enough to run through a colander to remove the seeds. Discard the seeds.

3 Combine the pulp, skins, sugar, raisins, and orange and lemon slices, and cook slowly until thickened. The mixture should coat the back of a wooden spoon, and form soft ridges as it slides off. If the mixture drips freely from the spoon it is not cooked enough. You may also place a few drops on a plate and place in the freezer for 3 to 5 minutes to see if it jells.

4 Once cooked, remove from the heat and stir in the chopped nuts. Pour the conserve into hot, sterilized half-pint jars, leaving ½ inch of headspace.

5 Seal with lids and process in a boiling water bath for 30 minutes (see note on page 195).

6 Wipe the jars and label them. Now line them up in a sunny window and watch the light shine through your treasures before tucking them away. Store in a cool, dark place and share with those you love most!

Strawberry Preserves
∼ *Stephanie Kimmel* ∼
MARCHÉ, EUGENE, OREGON

We'd be remiss if we didn't have a recipe for strawberry preserves in this chapter. Stephanie Kimmel's version is simple, although you do need special equipment—a canning kettle—to truly preserve the integrity of the fresh summer berries for use throughout the year. Enjoy these preserves on toast, swirled into oatmeal, or spread on a warm, freshly baked, buttered muffin.

MAKES ABOUT 3 PINTS

8 cups perfect strawberries, stemmed, but left whole

6 cups sugar

Juice of 1 large lemon, strained

1 Layer the strawberries in a ceramic or stainless steel bowl with the sugar, then turn with your hands to coat the berries evenly. Let the berries macerate for 6 hours or overnight in the refrigerator, covered. Gently turn them a few times to incorporate the sugar that falls to the bottom of the bowl. The idea is for the sugar to dissolve completely but to keep the berries as whole as possible.

2 With a rubber spatula, transfer the berries and syrup to a large flat skillet or preserving kettle. Add the lemon juice and bring to a boil. Let the mixture boil for a few minutes, stirring from time to time, then return to the bowl. Let cool, uncovered, then cover and let the mixture stand overnight in the refrigerator.

3 The next day, drain the syrup from the berries into the preserving pan and bring it to a boil. Cook until it reaches the jelly stage (220° F at sea level). Add the fruit and any liquid left in the bowl to the pan, and bring back to the boil. Stir gently until the syrup reaches the jelly stage again, about 5 minutes.

4 Remove the pan from the heat and skim any foam from the surface. Let it rest for about 5 minutes, stirring occasionally to keep the berries from floating to the top.

5 Ladle the preserves into hot, sterilized pint jars, leaving ½ inch of headspace (see note on page 195). Seal with lids and process in a boiling water bath for 15 minutes.

Aunt Sis's Tomato Preserves
❦ *Stephanie Kimmel* ❦
MARCHÉ, EUGENE, OREGON

These sweet-and-spicy preserved tomatoes are a surprising delight! It's unusual to find tomatoes preserved this way, and they're absolutely delicious. They are a nice addition to any pantry or gift basket. Stephanie loved them with fried eggs, grits, and sausage along with her aunt's fabulous biscuits. Late summer, when tomatoes are ripe, plentiful, and less expensive, is a great time to make these preserves.

MAKES ABOUT 3 PINTS

4 cups sugar

1 (1-inch) piece ginger, peeled and sliced into thin coins

1 (1-inch) piece cinnamon stick

1 lemon, thinly sliced

6 cups ripe tomatoes, cored, peeled, and quartered

1 In a large flat skillet or preserving kettle, combine ¾ cup of water and the sugar. Stir over low heat until the sugar is dissolved. Add the ginger, cinnamon, and lemon to the syrup and simmer for 15 to 20 minutes. Add the tomatoes and continue to simmer for another 15 minutes, stirring often to prevent sticking.

2 Let the mixture cool, uncovered, then cover and let it stand overnight in the refrigerator.

3 The next day, drain the syrup from the tomatoes into the skillet or kettle and bring it to a boil until it reaches the jelly stage (220° F at sea level). Add the tomatoes and any liquid left in the bowl to the pan, and bring back to a boil. Stir gently until the syrup reaches the jelly stage again, about 5 minutes.

4 Remove the pan from the heat and skim any foam from the surface. Remove the cinnamon stick. Let rest for about 5 minutes, stirring occasionally to keep the tomatoes and lemon from floating to the top.

5 Ladle the preserves into hot, sterilized pint jars, leaving ½ inch of headspace (see note on page 195). Seal with lids and process in a boiling water bath for 15 minutes.

Pantry Pickles
❧ *Susan Feniger* ❧
BORDER GRILL, SANTA MONICA AND LAS VEGAS
CIUDAD, LOS ANGELES

Susan Feniger's (pictured with her mother, opposite) Pantry Pickles aren't pickles in the traditional sense because they're not canned and have to be stored in the refrigerator, but they're an excellent choice (as are Sara Moulton's Pickled Red Onions, page 206) if you want to try pickling but aren't ready for the whole mysterious (yet surprisingly simple!) canning process. More than that, they're really good!

MAKES 1 GENEROUS QUART

6 pickling cucumbers or Kirbies
  (see Pantry Tip), with skins
1 onion, thinly sliced across the width
1 red bell pepper, cored, seeded, and
  julienned

2 cups rice wine vinegar *(see note)*
½ cup sugar
1 tablespoon kosher salt

Cut the cucumbers widthwise into ¹⁄₁₆-inch diagonal slices. Combine all of the ingredients in a medium saucepan. Bring to a boil, reduce to a simmer, and cook, uncovered, for 10 to 15 minutes. Store in pickling liquid in the refrigerator.

Mom's Secret Kirbies or pickling cucumbers are small, pale green cucumbers with fewer seeds and a milder flavor than larger cucumbers. They are available in supermarkets. Rice wine vinegar is a full-flavored, yellow Japanese vinegar made from rice wine. It's available in Asian markets and many supermarkets.

⊰ KITCHEN MEMORIES ⊱

My mother was a fantastic cook, absolutely fantastic! She was skinny as could be and would never eat much, but she was like a restaurant cook in that she would always taste things. She had a heavy hand with seasoning, so she really understood about putting in a lot of acidity and salt. Even though she used Lawry's and paprika, her food was always strongly flavored. She'd make fabulous fried chicken or a great chicken-and-artichoke casserole, and we always had great kugel around and brisket and pickled tongue and pot roast, and she'd make homemade applesauce and pancakes. She cooked and entertained a lot. She would never fail to have prepared food in the refrigerator, so if someone stopped over, she could put out things for people to snack on. If she made a salad, she made her own French dressing. She always did all this other great stuff to a salad so that it would be wonderful. She used tons of garnish, like marinated mushrooms, blue cheese, canned artichokes, and canned chickpeas in a salad. She wouldn't just make a salad with iceberg lettuce and nothing on it. And back in those days—forty or fifty years ago —it was pretty amazing that she was cooking and thinking about it like that.

Pickled Red Onions
Sara Moulton
GOURMET MAGAZINE, NEW YORK

Sara Moulton's family celebrates the New Year with Smoked Salmon and Salmon Roe on Crispy Potato Pancakes with Horseradish Cream (page 70), and these pickled onions are the recipe's crowning jewels. They also make a great addition to almost any salad or sandwich and keep well in the refrigerator for about a week.

MAKES ABOUT 2 CUPS

2 medium red onions, sliced ¼ inch thick
1½ cups cider vinegar
2 cloves garlic, peeled and halved

3 tablespoons sugar
1 tablespoon pickling spice
1½ teaspoons kosher salt

1 Combine the onion, cider vinegar, garlic, sugar, pickling spice, and salt in a saucepan and bring to a boil over high heat.

2 Reduce the heat to medium and simmer for 2 minutes. Remove from the heat and cool to room temperature. Chop fine before serving.

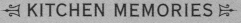

⫸ KITCHEN MEMORIES ⫷

Whenever anyone asks me why I became I chef, I always say it was because I love to eat. I'm always thinking about the next meal or the next year of meals! My mom was a very good cook, but for some crazy reason it only dawned on me a couple of years ago how extraordinary her cooking was when I was growing up in the fifties and sixties. She was making stuff like fresh artichokes, asparagus, endive, and shad roe. I recently said, "How the hell did you know about this stuff and how did you find it?!"

I grew up in New York City, and my mom started traveling when I was about seven years old. She'd always wanted to go to Europe. She'd go on a trip every year with her girlfriends and just loved it. Every time she went to a new country, she'd come home and make food from there, so I was constantly being exposed to new ingredients. Later my sister and I started going on some trips with her to England, Scotland, and France.

Every summer, with my aunt and uncle and their kids, we would share this farmhouse in northeastern Massachusetts down the road from my grandmother. Aunt Jean was a fabulous cook also—completely self-taught. We were up there every summer for three months. My aunt and uncle had three kids, my parents had three kids, and all the kids have had kids, so now it's become like a timeshare. It's crazy up there, but sometimes we're all up there at once—twenty-three or twenty-five people! So we have some great big feasts. My sister's a wonderful baker, her husband's a good cook. My brother's a good cook. His wife makes Italian food. My cousin married this Polish guy who is a phenomenal cook (except he uses too much sugar!). Then my cousin Josh went to the CIA and is also a chef. So up there, time is planned around food. We do as much exercise as we possibly can just so we can eat another big meal! My upbringing, and my children's upbringing have really been happy eating times.

Chapter Eight

Legacies

ONE OF THE MANY WAYS we can leave behind pieces of ourselves is through our cooking. Food is so sensual, so evocative, that it literally can transport a person back to a time and place with a single wispy, fleeting scent. All of the recipes in this book are included because they are parts of the histories of the families about whom we've written, and the recipes in this chapter are no exception.

Eve Felder is preserving her adopted children's Chinese culture and history with recipes like Chinese Braised Pork Shoulder and Chinese Kale; Gale Gand uses her mother Myrna's recipes (Myrna's Beef Shortribs and Grandma Myrna's Pancakes) to teach her children about their grandmother, whom they've never met; and Joyce Goldstein's Farro with Sweet Corn is something new she created for her grandchildren, who love it so much they suggested she send the recipe to us for this book. Food legacies can come from one's history or be created anew. We hope this chapter inspires you to make some of your own food legacies in a world that is losing its food history to processed, packaged, and fast foods.

Chardonnay and Cornmeal Cake
≈ *Anne Willan* ≈

Of late Anne Willan and her family have been making this cake quite frequently. Made in a food processor, it requires little effort and is an all-around great cake. As Anne says, "This New Age cake has everything: earthy flavor, rich golden color, and an unexpected crunch on the tongue. The longer you keep it, the moister it will be."

MAKES 1 SINGLE-LAYER CAKE

1½ cups all-purpose flour
4 teaspoons baking powder
½ teaspoon salt
⅔ cup coarse yellow cornmeal
⅔ cup flaked, blanched almonds

½ cup (1 stick) unsalted butter, diced
1 cup sugar
2 eggs, lightly beaten
1 cup full-flavored white wine
    (see note)

1 Preheat the oven to 350° F. Butter a single 9-inch cake pan, line the base with wax paper, butter the paper, then coat the pan with flour.

2 Sift the flour with the baking powder and salt in the bowl of a food processor. Add the cornmeal, almonds, butter, and sugar. Work the mixture, using the pulse button, until it forms crumbs that start to clump together, about 30 seconds.

3 Add the remaining ingredients and pulse just until smooth. Pour the batter into the cake pan and bake until the cake starts to shrink from the sides of the pan and springs back when lightly pressed with a fingertip, 45 to 55 minutes. Let the cake cool in the pan for about 10 minutes, then turn it onto a wire rack to cool completely. Serve it with fresh berries or fruit soup.

Mom's Secret For cooking, a punchy, concentrated chardonnay from Australia or California would be on target here, one of those large-scale whites "redolent with tropical fruit flavors," as wine writers like to say. For drinking, a glass of Italian vin santo might be nice with the crunchy almonds in this cake.

Country-Style Spring Chicken
with Onions, Potatoes, and Olives
Lidia Bastianich

FELIDIA & BECCO, NEW YORK
LIDIA'S ITALY, PITTSBURGH & KANSAS CITY, MISSOURI

This recipe is a favorite in Lidia's home and will no doubt go down in family history as one of her best dishes. She serves it in her restaurants and the guests love it as well. Lidia hopes that it will become a favorite in your home too.

SERVES 6

4 pounds young chicken parts
¼ cup extra virgin olive oil
Salt and freshly ground black pepper
   to taste
1½ pounds small (about 1½-inch-
   diameter) red potatoes, halved
3 small onions (about 6 ounces)

2 sprigs fresh rosemary
20 pitted Kalamata olives
1 whole pepperoncino (dried hot red
   pepper), broken in half, or
   ½ teaspoon crushed red pepper
2 tablespoons chopped Italian parsley

1 In a large bowl, toss the chicken pieces with the olive oil. Season with salt and pepper and toss again. Heat two large (at least 12-inch) nonstick or well-seasoned cast iron pans over medium heat. Add the chicken pieces, skin side down, and cover the skillets. Cook the chicken, turning it once, until golden brown on both sides, 5 to 7 minutes.

2 Move the chicken pieces to one side of the skillet. Add the potato halves, cut sides down, to the clear side of the skillet and cook on medium heat for 15 minutes, turning them and the chicken pieces often, until evenly browned. (At this point, both the chicken and potatoes should be crisp and brown.)

3 Reduce the heat to medium-low. Divide the onions, rosemary, olives, and pepperoncino between the skillets and cook, covered, until the onions have softened and the flavors have blended, about 15 minutes. Stir the contents of the skillets gently several times as they cook.

4 Drain the oil from the pan, sprinkle with chopped parsley, and serve.

Chinese Braised Pork Shoulder or Clay Pot Pork
≈ *Eve Felder* ≈

THE CULINARY INSTITUTE OF AMERICA, HYDE PARK, NEW YORK

Eve Felder, whose Southern roots run deep, adopted two beautiful little girls, Emma (pictured opposite, with Eve) and Genevieve, from China, and she enjoys teaching them about their cultural heritage. Her legacy to them is to educate them about all foods, but especially the food of their homeland. This Chinese Braised Pork Shoulder is one of their favorite recipes.

SERVES 10

½ **cup soy sauce**

½ **cup hoisin sauce**

2 **tablespoons black bean sauce**

1 **teaspoon salt**

1 **teaspoon black pepper**

2 **tablespoons sugar**

20 **thin slices peeled fresh ginger**

3 **pounds pork butt**

1 In a large mixing bowl, combine the soy sauce, hoisin sauce, black bean sauce, salt, pepper, sugar, and ginger. Mix well to combine. Add the pork and marinate overnight, in the refrigerator, or for at least 8 hours.

2 Preheat the oven to 250° F.

3 Place the pork into a Chinese clay pot (or a tightly covered Dutch oven). Slowly braise for 6 hours, until fork-tender.

Mom's Secret This pork is delicious served with rice and Chinese greens (see Chinese Kale, page 214), a staple for Eve's family. It's also delicious as a stuffing for suckling pig, shredded and added to Thai sticky rice with finely chopped Chinese greens and Chinese sausage. Eve says suckling pig is one of the most delicious celebration foods ever!

⊱ KITCHEN MEMORIES ⊰

It has been an absolute dream come true having my two little girls who are of Chinese heritage and being able to train them to have a connection to the earth and an appreciation of food. Not long ago, my three-year-old, Emma, was in the garden and peeking out of the snow was some mache. She actually recognized it and said, "Hey mom, here's some mache!" Their sense of discovery just takes my breath away. Last summer my youngest, Genevieve, was sitting in the middle of the garden. I was so excited because the first tomato, a green zebra, had just come out. I put it in my basket and went about tending the rest of the garden. Then I turned around and the child had eaten the entire thing! She is a fruitaholic. She will scream for red currants when I walk by the red currant bush. And she literally cannot get enough tomatoes in season. My daughters have inspired me, of course, to keep their culture alive, so I've found myself making sure that they have an appreciation for Chinese food, and making them proud of their heritage and the great gifts that their culture has provided to the world in terms of food connected with healing. We do a lot of talking about that and about eating good healthy food. Not long ago they were both suffering a little bit from a cold, so I made wontons and they had two giant bowls of wonton soup.

Chinese Kale

Eve Felder

THE CULINARY INSTITUTE OF AMERICA, HYDE PARK, NEW YORK

The pediatrician asked Eve's three-year-old daughter what her favorite food was and she replied, "kale." Since she is very long and lanky, the doctor wondered whether Eve was providing her with enough fat! This is another extremely flavorful dish that can be made with any hearty green, including collards, mustard greens, Swiss chard, or turnip greens—even spinach if it's cooked quickly.

SERVES 8

2 pounds kale	2 teaspoons sugar
2 tablespoons soy sauce	2 tablespoons oil
2 tablespoons oyster sauce	2 tablespoons finely minced fresh ginger
1 teaspoon salt	2 tablespoons finely minced garlic

1 Remove any coarse stems from the kale. Roll and cut into ¼-inch ribbons. Reserve.

2 Combine ¾ cup of water, the soy and oyster sauces, salt, and the sugar.

3 Heat the oil in a wok or large sauté pan. Add the ginger and garlic. Cook until the ginger and garlic release a pleasant aroma. Add the kale. Stir-fry until the kale begins to wilt.

4 Add the liquid ingredients. Cook for 20 to 30 minutes over moderate heat until the greens are tender to the bite. Add additional seasoning if necessary.

Myrna's Beef Shortribs
❧ Gale Gand ❧
TRU, CHICAGO

Gale Gand has such a wonderful sensibility about what it means to leave the legacy of food to her children that we just had to include as many of her recipes as we could. The two that follow are her mother's legacy, both to Gale and now to Gale's children, and they play a huge role in her current family life. Oh, and they're really good, too!

SERVES 8

3 pounds beef short ribs, cut up
Salt to taste
Freshly ground black pepper to taste
All-purpose flour as needed
2 tablespoons vegetable oil
1 medium onion, sliced
½ cup celery leaves
2 sprigs parsley

1½ cups beef stock or broth
2 cups canned diced tomato
6 medium carrots
8 small onions
4 medium potatoes or 2 parsnips
   (if you're serving this with mashed
   potatoes)
1 teaspoon paprika

1 Remove any excess fat from the ribs. Sprinkle them with salt and pepper and then roll them in flour.

2 In a Dutch oven, heat the vegetable oil and brown the short ribs on all sides. Add the sliced onions, celery leaves, parsley, and beef stock. Cover and simmer on low heat for 2 hours, or until the meat is very tender, adding more stock if needed.

3 Add the canned tomato, carrots, onions, potatoes or parsnips, and paprika, and season with a little salt and pepper. Continue cooking, covered, for another 30 minutes, or until the vegetables are tender. Serve family style on a very large platter.

Grandma Myrna's Pancakes
❧ Gale Gand ❧

TRU, CHICAGO

Gale (pictured below) calls these pancakes, but they're more like crêpes or blintzes. While Gale's mom filled them with peanut butter and jelly, all sorts of different sweet fillings can be used. The possibilities are virtually endless!

SERVES 4

2 eggs
½ cup milk
½ teaspoon salt
1 teaspoon sugar
½ cup all-purpose flour

Unsalted butter for the pan
1 cup peanut butter, smooth or chunky
½ cup blueberry jam or crabapple jelly
Confectioners' sugar for dusting

1 In a medium bowl, whisk together the eggs and milk. Whisk in the salt, sugar, and flour and set aside for 30 minutes to let the batter tenderize.

2 In a nonstick 10-inch skillet, melt about ½ teaspoon of butter over medium heat. When it foams, pour or ladle in about 2 tablespoons of batter. Lift and swirl the pan so the batter coats the bottom. Replace the pan on the burner and cook just until the crêpe is set and the underside is lightly browned. Using a spatula or your fingers, flip and cook until the other side is lightly browned. Transfer to a warmed platter. Repeat until the batter is used up.

3 One by one, spread each crêpe with a layer of 2 tablespoons peanut butter and 1 tablespoon blueberry jam and roll up like a cigar. Serve two per person, sprinkled with confectioners' sugar.

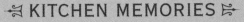 KITCHEN MEMORIES

My mother died before my son Gio was born. Though my mother hated being in the kitchen, she had a talent for it and it turns out that her entire identity, in my son's mind, is her food. It is the great truth that the way to eternal life is through your recipes and through passing on your dishes. We make "Grandma Myrna's Pancakes" every weekend. They're basically blintzes or crêpes, and it was my mother's blintz recipe that she made for my brother all the time. This was before Teflon, and if one got stuck to the pan and got torn, I would eat it because I didn't like them filled; I just wanted them with powdered sugar. I'd stand there next to my mother waiting for the torn ones. It was something special that we did together. Now my son and I make them together. He stands next to me just as I did with my mother. It started when he was maybe one and a half and could just barely pour the milk into a cup. As he's grown older he can do just about the whole thing, from whisking to ladling the batter into the pan and he's got the whole tilt of the pan, down. I still flip them. It's become a weekend ritual for us. It's the way that my son connects with his grandma, it's like a visit with her once a week. We talk and reminisce about her. The catalyst for starting a conversation about her is always a dish. There are other dishes, too, like her chicken paprikash, and her shortribs (page 215).

She wrote a lot of things down on recipe cards and even made chatty sidebar notes. It's almost as if she's talking to me. I'll read a note that will say, "Made this on Wednesday, September 6th, 1963. Didn't like the carrots. Next time try using parsnips." My grandma did the same thing on note cards, and I have them all in a little 3x5 file. I'm able to go back and look at these recipes and see their thoughts and their processes through it all. So, cooking with Gio not only helped to develop his fine and gross motor skills and his ability to pour and measure, but it also connected him with these other generations. It's the only way he knows my mom.

Simply A'Maize'ing Corn Ice Cream
Loretta Barrett Oden
CORN DANCE CAFÉ, SANTA FE, NEW MEXICO

Loretta remembers learning to cook with her mother, aunts, and grandmother. There were always women in the kitchen laughing and singing. One of her most vivid memories is of foraging for possum grapes and sand plums with her aunts. Afterward, they would all get together and compete to see who could make the clearest jelly. County and state fairs were other venues for their fun-loving competitive spirits. "It was just wonderful," she recalls, "the camaraderie, the laughing, the singing, and all of that in the kitchen!"

She came to the foodservice business quite late in life by comparison with most of the other chefs in this book. At forty-eight she found herself divorced and in need of a profession, so at the age of fifty she opened The Corn Dance Café in Santa Fe, New Mexico. It felt like a natural thing for her to do, and she remembers thinking that it would be great— like a neverending dinner party. The restaurant has been an overwhelming success.

Half Potawatomi Indian and half English and Irish, Loretta has dedicated herself to the promotion of Native American food, indigenous ingredients, and teaching the next generation the importance of both, as she herself had been taught. She is currently working on a PBS Series entitled *Seasoned with Spirit: A Native Cook's Journey*. This ice cream recipe is one of her favorites.

MAKES 2 QUARTS

2½ cups fresh, sweet corn kernels
   (4 or 5 medium ears)
3 cups heavy cream
1½ cups milk

¼ teaspoon salt
10 egg yolks
1 cup raw sugar
1½ teaspoons vanilla extract

1 In a saucepan, combine 2 cups of corn and ½ cup of heavy cream. Cook until the corn is just tender, 3 or 4 minutes. Place in a blender or food processor and puree until smooth. Set aside.

2 Over medium heat, combine 1½ cups of the cream, the milk, and the salt. Bring to a boil, then remove from the heat. Set aside.

3 Combine the egg yolks, sugar, and reserved corn purée. Whisk in the remaining 1 cup of cream and the remaining ½ cup of whole corn kernels. Cook over low heat, stirring constantly, until the mixture coats the back of a spoon, about 10 minutes. Do not allow the mixture to come to a boil. Remove from the heat, stir in the warm cream mixture, and add the vanilla extract. Cool to room temperature, cover tightly, and refrigerate until cold. Pour the mixture into an ice cream maker and freeze.

Mom's Secret As a variation, try adding some fresh fruit to this mixture at the end of the freezing process. Berries can be left whole and other fruits should be diced according to your preference. If the fruit is not very ripe and sweet, you may need to add a bit more sugar to the recipe. Loretta's favorites are bananas, fresh ripe peaches, and mango.

In the interest of increasing the corn flavor, Loretta often makes a corn stock by simmering the corncobs in a stockpot for many hours and then reducing the resulting liquid. She substitutes the corn stock for a portion of the heavy cream and milk. Interestingly, there was no dairy in the Americas before European contact. Slightly fermented corn (maize) was also used as a natural sweetener by many native people.

Jennifer's Scones
Cindy Pawlcyn

CINDY'S BACKSTREET KITCHEN, ST. HELENA, CALIFORNIA
MUSTARDS GRILL, YOUNTVILLE, CALIFORNIA

These wonderful, traditional scones are part of the legacy bestowed upon Cindy Pawlcyn by her stepchildren, Peter and Kirstie (pictured opposite), who are of Scottish descent. Kirstie's favorite way to eat them was sprinkled with orange-colored sugar, and Cindy always enjoyed watching the two kids devour an entire batch by themselves in less than fifteen minutes.

MAKES 12 TO 16 SCONES

1 cup currants
4 cups all-purpose flour
⅓ cup sugar
4 teaspoons baking powder
½ teaspoon baking soda

1 teaspoon salt
6 ounces (1½ sticks) butter
2 egg yolks
¾ cup cream
1 cup sour cream

1 Preheat the oven to 350° F.

2 Mix the currants, flour, sugar, baking powder, baking soda, and salt. Cut in the butter until the mixture is crumbly, as you would for pie dough.

3 Combine the egg yolks, cream, and sour cream and add to the flour mixture. Mix as briefly as possible to combine. Do not overmix.

4 Divide the dough into 2 equal pieces. Pat out into 1½-inch-thick circles. Cut into 6 or 8 pie-shaped pieces (depending on how large you want them).

5 On a cookie sheet, bake for 15 to 18 minutes or until golden. Serve with lightly sweetened whipped cream and fresh strawberries, or strawberry jam, or all three.

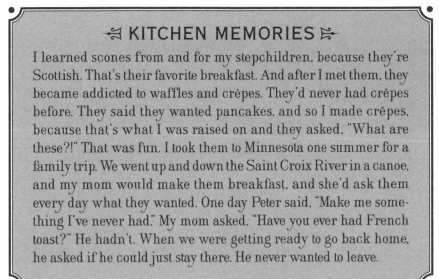

⧯ KITCHEN MEMORIES ⧯

I learned scones from and for my stepchildren, because they're Scottish. That's their favorite breakfast. And after I met them, they became addicted to waffles and crêpes. They'd never had crêpes before. They said they wanted pancakes, and so I made crêpes, because that's what I was raised on and they asked, "What are these?!" That was fun. I took them to Minnesota one summer for a family trip. We went up and down the Saint Croix River in a canoe, and my mom would make them breakfast, and she'd ask them every day what they wanted. One day Peter said, "Make me something I've never had." My mom asked, "Have you ever had French toast?" He hadn't. When we were getting ready to go back home, he asked if he could just stay there. He never wanted to leave.

Summer Berry Shortbread Tartlettes
❧ *Debbie Gold* ❧
40 SARDINES, OVERLAND PARK, KANSAS

Debbie doesn't know how she ever became interested in cooking because as a child growing up in the Chicago area, she wasn't exposed to any very interesting foods. Her family's meals were simple and largely uninspired. Even as a child, though, Debbie had an innate interest in baking from scratch. As she got more experienced in the kitchen, her mother would let her cook dinner for the family.

In college she enrolled in a restaurant management degree program and applied for a job at a local restaurant. Being an inexperienced kid from the suburbs, she had no idea how to dress for the interview, so she got all dolled up. The chef, naturally, was skeptical and warned her that she might break a nail. She assured him that she wasn't worried about that, and he finally hired her to be an expeditor in the summer. Later, Debbie got an apprenticeship in France, taking cooking classes at a trade school about an hour south of Lyon and working at some of the finer area restaurants, including Michel Chabron and Le Gourmandin.

When she returned to Chicago in 1987, she worked at Charlie Trotter's, where she met her husband, Michael Smith. The two worked in France and Kansas City and had two children, Misha and Sophie (pictured above). Then in 2001 these two Beard Award winners opened their own place, 40 Sardines. Debbie cooks all the time with her little girls, and one of their absolute favorite things is these Summer Berry Shortbread Tartlettes.

Mom's Secret These tartlettes can be made with whatever fruit you enjoy most. Plums, peaches, and apricots can be substituted for berries. In the fall or winter, try sautéed pears or apples. Pastry cream with a crumble topping is another great combination.

2 cups plus 2 tablespoons all-purpose
    flour
1¼ cups confectioners' sugar
Pinch salt
½ pound (2 sticks) unsalted butter, cold,
    cut into cubes
1 egg

1 teaspoon vanilla extract
½ cup lemon curd
1 cup of your favorite summer berries
    (raspberries, blueberries,
    blackberries)
Whipped cream or crème fraîche
    for garnish

1 Sift the dry ingredients together into a large mixing bowl. Cut in the butter until the mixture resembles coarse meal. In a separate bowl, whisk together the egg and vanilla. Add to the flour mixture and mix until the dough forms a ball. Remove the dough from bowl and wrap in plastic. Chill the dough overnight or for a minimum of 2 hours.

2 Preheat the oven to 350° F. Remove the dough from the refrigerator. Cut it into 1-inch cubes. Roll the cubes into balls. Place each ball in a 2-ounce muffin-tin-cups. Make an indentation in the center of the ball with your thumb. Dollop about 1 teaspoon of lemon curd in the indentation. Place four or five berries on top.

3 Bake for 15 minutes, just until golden. Let cool. The tartlettes should pop right out. Serve them with a little crème fraîche or whipped cream.

❧ KITCHEN MEMORIES ❧

Misha, my oldest daughter, likes to make salad. A lot of people are worried about knives and kids, but I give her a little paring knife, and she likes to cut the radishes and cucumber and tear salad. I'll take pork tenderloin, make medallions, and let the girls pound them out. I love to be interactive with them. I let them do the shortbread tartlettes with their hands at home. The first time we did it their hands were just covered with dough and they turned to me as if to say, "Mom what do we do?" I said, "Oh, those are way too dirty, you're going to have to lick those off," and their eyes just widened in disbelief. We also make almond cake together. I'll get things started by roughly chopping the almonds, and then I put them in a Ziploc bag and hand each of them a rolling pin and let them pound away. When we make lemon meringue pie, I pipe the meringue on the pie and let them practice on the countertop with the leftover meringue.

Farro with Sweet Corn
~ *Joyce Goldstein* ~

Farro is a whole grain, an early wheat variety that has a nutty taste, sort of like barley. It can be found in health food stores and near the rice in many supermarkets. Joyce's grandchildren's favorite way to eat farro is combined with corn, so she makes it often. Joyce says that "they love the contrast of the two small round shapes with different textures, the chewiness of the farro, and the crunch of the corn." It makes a good accompaniment to roast chicken, lamb chops, etc.

SERVES 6

2 cups farro, rinsed

2 to 3 cups corn kernels, blanched and
   refreshed in cold water (about 3 ears)

2 tablespoons chopped flat leaf parsley

2 tablespoons chopped chives

Salt and freshly ground black pepper
   to taste

Unsalted butter to taste

1 Bring 6 cups of salted water to a boil and add the farro. Cover the pot and simmer over low heat until tender, about 25 minutes. The farro doubles in volume after cooking. Start checking for doneness after 20 minutes. When cooked, it will be tender but still have some chewiness at the center. A bit of water may remain unabsorbed, but if the farro is too wet, drain it in a strainer and then return it to the pot.

2 Fold in the corn, the herbs, salt and pepper, and butter to taste. Warm through over very low heat.

⇥ KITCHEN MEMORIES ⇤

I love to cook for friends and family. When the little ones are interested, it's really exciting. I remember the first time I made farro for them and put little fresh corn niblets in it. My grandson was so excited to have this new thing he said, "Oh, I love this carro, Grandma,"—he combined the two words and it was just so darling. Teaching table manners is also fun. I was always trained at home about how to have good table manners, and I think it's an important part of the ritual of dining together that should continue to be passed on to the next generations.

Christmas Cake
❦ *Hilary Demane* ❧
INDIANA UNIVERSITY OF PENNSYLVANIA (IUP), INDIANA, PENNSYLVANIA

Hilary assures us that she's heard all the fruitcake jokes and wants to go on record as saying that she admits there's a lot of bad fruitcake out there. However, she urges you, as she does her students, to withhold judgment until you've tasted this one. We agree. This is great fruitcake!

Hilary is well known for this cake, and we daresay it will become part of her legacy whether she intends it to or not. Her family is filled with "fruitcake fiends," and the one and only gift they insist upon from Hilary is her fruitcake, because it's a taste of their past. She certainly hears about it if she doesn't make fruitcake for Christmas! Of course, you don't have to celebrate Christmas to enjoy the wonderful flavors and textures of this special cake.

MAKES 4 STANDARD LOAVES

1 pound golden raisins

1 pound dark raisins

1 pound glacé cherries

1 pound glacé pineapple

½ cup glacé orange peel

¼ cup glacé lemon peel

¼ cup glacé citron (if you don't like the green candied fruit in your Christmas cake, omit this)

12 ounces coarsely chopped blanched almonds

12 ounces walnut halves

¾ cup dark rum, plus additional to taste

¼ cup brandy, plus additional to taste

1½ cups (3 sticks) unsalted butter, at room temperature

1 pound light brown sugar

1 cup granulated sugar

12 large eggs, at room temperature

1½ teaspoons almond extract

½ teaspoon lemon extract

2 teaspoons vanilla extract

5½ cups all-purpose flour (or 14 ounces bread flour and 14 ounces cake flour if available)

1 teaspoon baking soda

½ teaspoon ground mace

½ teaspoon ground nutmeg, preferably freshly grated

⊰ KITCHEN MEMORIES ⊱

I have wonderful memories of making this a family tradition every year with everyone taking a turn at stirring (for good luck in the New Year), just as our English ancestors would have. It was baked in November after Thanksgiving and unveiled for the festivities at Christmas and New Years, served up with rich eggnog laced with rum and lots of happy toasting to the future and stories about the past.

1 Toss the fruit and nuts with the rum and brandy and cover for 2 hours or preferably overnight, stirring occasionally. This does not need refrigeration.

2 Cream the butter and both sugars with the paddle attachment on medium speed for approximately 20 minutes, scraping often, until light in color and texture. Preheat the oven to 325° F.

3 Add the eggs, one at a time, blending and scraping between additions, then add the extracts.

4 Sift the flour with the baking soda and dry spices and fold into the batter by hand.

5 Add the macerated fruit and nuts to the batter and fold in to incorporate. There should be just enough batter to coat the fruit; remember, the fruit is the star in this cake.

6 Prepare your loaf or tube pans by coating them generously with shortening and dusting them with flour. You may also brush with a commercial depanner, but spray coatings are not advised as they may stick.

7 Fill the pans two-thirds full and tap gently to remove any air pockets. Decorate the tops with candied cherries, pineapple, walnut halves, or peel if you desire.

8 Bake for 45 minutes to 1½ hours, depending on the size of the pans. Check for doneness with a toothpick: It should come out clean but moist. Let the cakes cool in the pan for 15 to 30 minutes, then remove them from the pans carefully and cool on a rack.

9   Once the cakes have cooled to room temperature, gently wrap them in cheesecloth and sprinkle them liberally with more dark rum or brandy. The cheesecloth should be very damp but not dripping wet. Wrap each cake in foil and refrigerate for 4 to 6 weeks, allowing them to age. This is an essential step to really great fruitcake. These can last for up to 1 year, refrigerated, without a loss of quality as long if properly wrapped and sealed.

Mom's Secret You can personalize this fruitcake to your tastes. Hilary has often substituted part dried fruit such as apricots, plums, dates, and currants, and nuts such as hazelnuts or pecans. She just recommends that you keep the total fruit-and-nut weight the same as in the original recipe.

10   When ready to serve, remove the foil and cheesecloth and slice with a sharp blade. (Clean it with hot water and wipe between each cut.) Fruitcake is always easier to cut when refrigerated and should be served in thin slices because of the rich flavors.

Index of Chefs' Restaurants

Jody Adams (54, 180)
RIALTO
The Charles Hotel
One Bennett Street
Cambridge, MA
617-661-5050

BLU
4 Avery Street
Boston, MA
617-375-8550

Fay Arolithianakis (146)
THOM THOM
3340 Park Avenue
Wantagh, NY
516-221-9022

Lidia Bastianich
(30, 84, 211)
FELIDIA
243 East 58th Street
New York, NY
212-758-1488

BECCO
355 West 46th Street
New York, NY
212-397-7597

LIDIA'S ITALY
101 West 22nd Street
Kansas City, MO
816-221-3722

LIDIA'S ITALY
1400 Smallman Street
Pittsburgh, PA
412-552-0150

Deann Bayless (86, 134)
FRONTERA GRILL /
TOPOLOBAMPO
445 North Clark Street
Chicago, IL
312-661-1434

Ann Cashion (32)
CASHION'S EAT PLACE
1819 Columbia Street
Washington, DC
202-797-1819

JOHNNY'S HALF SHELL
2002 P Street, NW
Washington, DC
202-296-2021

Gloria Ciccarone-Nehls
(90)
HUNTINGTON HOTEL
1075 California Street
San Francisco, CA
415-474-5400

Traci Des Jardins
(118, 120)
JARDINIERE
300 Grove Street
San Francisco, CA
415-861-5555

ACME CHOPHOUSE
24 Willie Mays Plaza
San Francisco, CA
415-644-0240

MIJITA
1 Ferry Building
(Embarcadero)
San Francisco, CA
415-399-0814

Gale Gand
(46, 48, 171, 191, 215, 216)
TRU
676 North St. Clair Street
Chicago, IL
312-202-0001

Debbie Gold (222)
40 SARDINES
11942 Roe Avenue
Overland Park, KS
913-451-1040

Kerry L. Heffernan
(21, 44)
THE FAIRMONT HOTEL
950 Mason Street
San Francisco, CA
415-772-5000

Katy Keck (66, 168, 192)
THE NEW WORLD GRILL
454 West 46th Street
New York, NY
212-957-4745

Stephanie Kimmel
(164, 202, 203)
MARCHÉ
296 East 5th Street
Eugene, OR
541-342-3612

Anita Lo (116)
ANNISA
13 Barrow Street
New York, NY
212-741-6699

Emily Luchetti (150, 178)
FARALLON
450 Post Street
San Francisco, CA
415-956-6969

Zarela Martinez (100, 102)
ZARELA RESTAURANT
953 Second Avenue
New York, NY
212-644-6740

Mary Sue Milliken (166)
Susan Feniger (179, 204)
BORDER GRILL
1445 4th Street
Santa Monica, CA
310-451-1655

BORDER GRILL
3950 Las Vegas Boulevard
South
Las Vegas, NV
702-632-7403

CIUDAD
445 South Figueroa Street
Los Angeles, CA
213-486-5171

Longteine de Monteiro
(18, 20)
Nadsa de Monteiro-Perry
(50)
ELEPHANT WALK
900 Beacon Street
Boston, MA
617-247-1500

ELEPHANT WALK
2067 Massachusetts Avenue
Cambridge, MA
617-492-6900

CARAMBOLA
663 Main Street
Waltham, MA
781-899-2244

Cindy Pawlcyn (24, 220)
CINDY'S BACKSTREET
KITCHEN
1327 Railroad Avenue
St. Helena, CA
707-963-1200

MUSTARDS GRILL
7399 St. Helena Highway
Yountville, CA
707-944-2424

Debra Ponzek (182)
AUX DELICES FOODS
1075 East Putnam Avenue
Riverside, CT
203-698-1066

Nora Pouillon (108, 124)
RESTAURANT NORA
2132 Florida Avenue, NW
Washington, DC
202-462-5143

ASIA NORA
2213 M Street, NW
Washington, DC
202-797-4860

Anne Quatrano (36)
BACCHANALIA/
STAR PROVISIONS
1198 Howell Mill Road
Atlanta, GA
404-365-0410

THE FLOATAWAY CAFÉ
1123 Zonolite Road Suite 15
Atlanta, GA
404-892-1414

Amy Scherber (174, 176)
AMY'S BREAD
75 Ninth Avenue
New York, NY
212-462-4338

Lisa Schroeder
(26, 104, 138, 188)
MOTHER'S BISTRO & BAR
409 SW Second Avenue
Portland, OR
503-464-1122

Ana Sortun (28)
OLEANA
134 Hampshire Street
Cambridge, MA
617-661-0505

Alice Waters (38)
CHEZ PANISSE
1517 Shattuck Avenue
Berkeley, CA
510-548-5525

CAFÉ FANNY
1603 San Pablo Avenue
Berkeley, CA
510-524-5447

Lucia Watson (52, 78)
LUCIA'S RESTAURANT
& WINE BAR
1432 West 31st Street
Minneapolis, MN
612-825-1572

Patricia Williams
(49, 142)
MORRELLS RESTAURANT
900 Broadway
New York, NY
212-253-0900

Sherry Yard (160, 162)
SPAGO
176 North Canon Drive
Beverly Hills, CA
310-385-0880

Index